Springer Books on Professional Computing

Edited by Henry Ledgard

Springer Books on Professional Computing

Computer Confidence: A Human Approach to Computers
Bruce D. Sanders. viii, 90 pages. 23 figures. 1984. ISBN 0-387-90917-6

The Unix System Guidebook: An Introductory Guide for Serious Users
Peter P. Sylvester. xi, 207 pages. 6 figures. 1984. ISBN 0-387-90906-0

The American Pascal Standard: With Annotations
Henry Ledgard. vii, 97 pages. 1984. ISBN 0-387-91248-7

The American Pascal Standard

With Annotations

Prepared by

Henry Ledgard

Springer-Verlag

New York Berlin Heidelberg Tokyo

Henry Ledgard
Drummer Hill Road, RFD 3
Amherst, MA 01002
U.S.A.

Series Editor
Henry Ledgard

(C.R.) Computer Classification: D.3.3

Library of Congress Cataloging in Publication Data
Ledgard, Henry F.
   The American Pascal standard.
   (Springer books on professional computing)
   Includes index.
   1. PASCAL (Computer program language)–Standards–
United States. I. Title. II. Series.
QA76.73.P2L393   1984   001.64'24   83-27150

ANSI/IEEE 770X3.97-1983 has been reprinted by permission of the American National Standards Institute and the Institute of Electrical and Electronics Engineers.

The annotations in this work represent the views of Dr. Henry Ledgard; they do not necessarily reflect the intent of the joint ANSI X3/IEEE Pascal committee.

For distribution in North America only.

Printed and bound by Halliday Litho, West Hanover, Massachusetts.
Printed in the United States of America.

9 8 7 6 5 4 3 2 1

ISBN 0-387-91248-7 Springer-Verlag New York Berlin Heidelberg Tokyo
ISBN 3-540-91248-7 Springer-Verlag Berlin Heidelberg New York Tokyo

PREFACE

The programming language Pascal has, over the years, achieved a remarkable success. The language has grown in popularity despite the lack of major industry or government backing. Part of its success is certainly due to its relatively small size and a certain elegance of design. It has virtually replaced its now ancient predecessor, Algol 60.

As the result of an international standard effort for Pascal, it is likely that the language will now achieve a stability among implementations. In this work we reproduce the American National Standard definition of Pascal, with annotations. This definition, officially known as ANSI/IEEE 770 X3.97-1983, was released by the American National Standards Institute (ANSI) and the Institute of Electrical and Electronic Engineers (IEEE).

The standard has been produced in cooperation with the International Organization for Standardization (ISO) and the British Standards Institution (BSI). Unfortunately, there are two versions of the Pascal standard, the American version (given here) and an international version. The international version is known as ISO 7185 and in Britain as BS 6192. The international standard defines the language Pascal in two levels: level 0 (the basic language) and level 1 (the basic language plus conformant arrays). The inclusion of conformant arrays in the international standard has been a matter of lively debate. The American version of the standard includes only level 0 of the international standard. The American and international versions also have a few minor differences. Fundamentally, however, the American standard and the international standard (level 0) are the same. They both cover the full Pascal language as originally proposed by Niklaus Wirth.

My objective in preparing this work has been twofold: first, to present the Pascal standard itself with an eye to its printed appearance, and second, to assist the reader in its comprehension. My objective was *not* to provide a definitive work on the details of Pascal, but rather to help reduce the mental effort needed to understand the standard.

In preparing the annotated standard presented here, consideration of human readability has been paramount. In particular, I have made use of a special typesetting font for programs, have adopted a slightly different style of BNF productions, and have reformatted the program examples. The annotations mainly provide examples, mention of tricky cases, and exposition of some difficult wordings. All of this is part of my general

disposition that much, much greater things can be done in computers to meet the human user half way.

Andy Mickel and Jim Miner provided thoughtful reviews of this work. Jon Hueras, a master of Pascal, provided a clutch homerun in the eighth inning; I sincerely appreciate their help.

Henry Ledgard
Drummer Hill Road
Amherst, Massachusetts

CONTENTS

AMERICAN STANDARD DEFINITION
of the
COMPUTER PROGRAMMING LANGUAGE

PASCAL

FOREWORD

(This Foreword is not a part of ANSI/IEEE 770 X3.97-1983, IEEE Standard Pascal Computer Programming Language.)

This standard provides an unambiguous and machine independent definition of the language Pascal. Its purpose is to facilitate portability of Pascal programs for use on a wide variety of data processing systems.

LANGUAGE HISTORY

The computer programming language Pascal was designed by Professor Niklaus Wirth to satisfy two principal aims:

(1) to make available a language suitable for teaching programming as a systematic discipline based on certain fundamental concepts clearly and naturally reflected by the language.

(2) to define a language whose implementations could be both reliable and efficient on then available computers.

However, it has become apparent that Pascal has attributes that go far beyond these original goals. It is now being increasingly used commercially in the writing of both system and application software. This standard is primarily a consequence of the growing commercial interest in Pascal and the need to promote the portability of Pascal programs between data processing systems.

In drafting this standard the continued stability of Pascal has been a prime objective. However, apart from changes to clarify the specification, one major change has been introduced. The syntax used to specify procedural and functional parameters has been changed to require the use of a procedure or function heading, as appropriate (see 6.6.3.1); this change was introduced to overcome a language insecurity. [1]

PROJECT HISTORY

(Throughout, the JPC refers to the Joint ANSI/X3J9-IEEE Pascal Standards Committee.) In the fall of 1978 application was made to the IEEE

[1]. Pascal is a language that is said to be "strongly typed". That is, each name has an associated type and the use of the name in various contexts can be checked to see if the usage is type-wise correct. For procedure and function parameters, the original definition of Pascal said nothing about their ex-

pected types of arguments. As a result, for example, a procedure parameter might in one place be associated with a procedure taking integer arguments and in another with a procedure taking the names of the days of the week as arguments. This is the "insecurity" mentioned in the standard. The solution, requiring a full procedure or function heading for the parameter, solves the problem albeit at some additional language complexity.

2. Without taking sides, it is unfortunate that the two bodies could not agree on a *single* standard, with no versions or levels.

Standards Board by the IEEE Computer Society to authorize project P770. After approval, the first meeting was held in January 1979.

In December of 1978, X3J9 convened as a result of a SPARC resolution to form a US TAG (Technical Advisory Group) for the ISO Pascal standardization effort initiated by the UK.

In agreement with IEEE representatives, in February of 1979, an X3 resolution combined the X3J9 and P770 committees into a single committee called the Joint ANSI/X3J9-IEEE Pascal Standards Committee. The first meeting as JPC was held in April 1979.

At its 7th meeting in April 1980, JPC reviewed the first draft of ISO dp7185 and submitted its technical comments as JPC/80-111 together with their recommendation to X3 that the US should vote "no, because" in light of these comments.[2]

For a summary of other important events in the project's history, see the annual reports from 1979 through 1981. Two other significant events occurred in February 1981:

(1) JPC reviewed the second draft of ISO dp7185 and submitted its technical comments as JPC/81-42 together with their recommendations to X3 that the US should vote "yes, but" in light of those comments.

(2) JPC passed a motion to submit to TC letter ballot the ISO dp7185 second draft together with JPC/81-42 and JPC/81-41 which describes how the requirements for compliance with the dpANS and proposed IEEE Pascal standard differ from compliance with the ISO draft proposed standard.

PROJECT CHARTER

As X3J9, it approved SD-3 described its program of work to be:

(1) Maintain a liaison with the ISO, BSI, and IEEE committees to work toward a common working draft standard. This work should include review of those bodies' documents and forwarding of comments based on that review. The eventual draft proposed American National Standard Pascal shall be compatible with any ISO Pascal standard and identical in content with the jointly developed proposed IEEE Pascal standard.

(2) Provide a means for review of all Pascal standardization activities.

(3) Carry out the development of a Pascal standard.

(4) Identify and evaluate common existing practices in the area of Pascal extensions.

(5) Act as a liaison group with organizations interested in interpretation of American National Standard Pascal.

The resolution to form JPC clarified the dual function of the single joint committee to produce a dpANS and a proposed IEEE Pascal standard, identical in content.

TECHNICAL DEVELOPMENT

(1) *Technical Constraints by X3 or IEEE.* None.

(2) *Technical Alternatives Considered.* In view of the charter to maintain compatibility with "any ISO Pascal standard," technical alternatives, suggestions, and recommendations were submitted with US letter ballots on ISO draft proposals. These items were then resolved by Working Group 4 as part of the international standardization process.

(3) *Significant Technical Issues on which JPC was Initially Divided.* Divergent opinions on the technical issues concerning conformant arrays [3] were forwarded as part of the US letter ballot comments (JPC/80-111, JPC/81-42). To resolve the issue within the JPC, the conformant arrays definition was removed from the proposed domestic standard. Therefore, extensions to the language that solve the conformant array issue are permitted in the same manner as any other extension.

(4) *Information Collection Techniques Employed to Obtain Broader Input Data.*
Working Draft 3 published April 1979 in IEEE Computer magazine.
Working Draft 3 published January 1979 in Pascal News No. 14
dp7185 First Draft published April 1980 in SIGPLAN Notices
dp7185 First Draft published May 1980 in Pascal News No. 18
dp7185 Second Draft published December 1980 in Pascal News No. 20.
Comments received from public review were distributed to all JPC members and discussed as part of the technical review. These were also forwarded directly to the appropriate international body responsible for an ISO dp.

(5) *Related Domestic Effort.* X3J9 (an X3 Technical Committee) and IEEE P770 combined to form the Joint ANSI/X3J9-IEEE Pascal Standards Committee in early 1979. The joint collaboration contributed in the international development of ISO/7185, from which this standard was developed.

INTERNATIONAL

The British Standards Institution (BSI) Committee OIS/5 has been our counterpart in the UK. They are the sponsoring body for the ISO dp for Pascal. There are similar active groups in Australia, Canada, France,

3. The original definition of Pascal required that the bounds of a formal array parameter be fixed. Hence functions and procedures called with arrays of varying lengths could not be written. The inclusion of "conformant" array parameters in the international standard solves this problem but with a definite increase in language complexity. This surely was a controversial point in drafting the standard. As a result the international standard is in two levels: level 0 (without conformant arrays) and level 1 (with conformant arrays). The American standard does not have conformant arrays.

4. The conformant array feature goes as follows. Consider a function SUM having a single parameter, a conformant array, as in

```
function SUM(A:array [I..J:INTEGER] of INTEGER):
   { -- returns } INTEGER;
   var
      COUNT: INTEGER;
begin
   SUM := 0;
   for COUNT := I to J do
      SUM := SUM + A[COUNT]
end;
```

Now consider the declarations

```
var
   SHORTARRAY: array [1..10]   of INTEGER;
   LONGARRAY:  array [1..1000] of INTEGER;
   CHARARRAY:  array [1..120]  of CHAR;
```

The statements

```
RESULT1 := SUM(SHORTARRAY)
RESULT2 := SUM(LONGARRAY)
```

would be legal, and the array bounds would be those of the actual parameter. On the other hand

```
RESULT := SUM(CHARARRAY)
```

would not be legal since the type of the components of CHARARRAY does not match those of the parameter A.

Germany, Netherlands and Japan. The international liaisons on these committees have been kept informed of the US activity by being on the JPC mailing list. Also, these committees have assigned members to WG4, the international working group for Pascal.

Other standards and their relationship to the American National Standard and IEEE Pascal Standard

ISO Pascal Standard. See the preceding section on Project Charter and the following section on Differences.

Differences of technical substance between this standard and the international standard, as represented by ISO/DIS 7185

The differences of technical substance are:

(1) The domestic standard does not include the conformant array feature.[4]

(2) The domestic standard specifies that extensions may alter the status of implementation-dependent features or errors. The ISO document prohibits extensions from altering the status of these items.

(3) The domestic standard specifies that the relationship, if any, between end-of-line and values of the char-types shall be implementation-dependent. The ISO document requires that end-of-line not be a value of the char-type.

(4) This standard specifies the ordering of evaluation, accessing, and binding of the parameters of READ, READLN, WRITE, and WRITELN. The international standard does not address these areas, leaving it neither specified, implementation-defined, nor implementation-dependent.

At the time of adoption of this standard, the text of the international standard was observed to contain several errors of definition and several points of apparent technical ambiguity or lack of clarity. This standard embodies corrections to those errors, and embodies certain wording which clarifies the apparent ambiguities. These differences in manner of definition are not differences of technical substance.

The errors that are corrected in this standard are in the definition of:

(1) String-element alternatives
(2) Data-transfer procedure parameters types
(3) Lexicographic ordering
(4) Control-variable usage restrictions

The international standard appears to permit or require the repeated evaluation of the file that is referenced by I/O procedures and of the arrays that are referenced by the data-transfer procedures. A detailed analysis is required to determine that the international standard does not in fact permit such repeated evaluation. This standard states that requirement more explicitly.

Except as noted in the list above of Differences of Technical Substance, compliance with this standard is equivalent to compliance at level 0 with the international standard in the following sense:

(1) Any program complying with this standard complies at level 0 with the international standard.

(2) Any program or processor complying at level 0 with the international standard complies with this standard. [5]

(3) Any processor complying at level 1 with the international standard complies with this standard if it is "able to process in a manner similar to that specified for errors any use of [the conformant-array feature]."

(4) Any processor complying with this standard and not providing an extension which covers part or all of the intent of the conformant-array feature complies at level 0 with the international standard.

(5) Any processor complying with this standard and providing an extension covering part or all of the intent of the conformant-array feature complies at level 1 with the international standard if it also includes the conformant-array feature.

Additionally, a program which uses any extension does not comply with either standard.

FUTURE WORK

An SD3 for extended Pascal has been approved by X3 to authorize future work.

Suggestions for the improvement of this standard are welcomed. These suggestions should be sent to:

Secretary
IEEE Standards Board
345 East 47th Street
New York, NY 10017

When the IEEE Standards Board approved this standard on September 17, 1981, it had the following membership:

I.N. Howell, Jr., *Chairman*   Irving Kolodny, *Vice Chairman*
                    Sava I. Sherr, *Secretary*

G.Y.R. Allen	Jay Forster	F. Rosa
J.J. Archambault	Kurt Greene	R.W. Seelbach
H.H. Beall	Loering M. Johnson	J.S. Stewart

[5]. Aside from the conformant array feature, the American and international standards are virtually identical. In almost all cases, the wording, organization, equations, and examples are identical.

J.T. Boettger	Joseph L. Koepfinger	W.E. Vannah
Edward Chelotti	J.E. May	Virginius N. Vaughan, Jr.
Edward J. Cohen	Donald T. Michael	Art Wall
Len S. Corey	J.P. Riganati	Robert E. Weiler

This standard was processed and approved for submittal to ANSI by the American National Standards Committee on Information Systems, X3. Committee approval of this standard does not necessarily imply that all committee members voted for its approval.

At the time it approved this standard, the X3 committee had the following members:

John F. Auwaerter, *Chairman*   J.A.N. Lee, *Vice Chairman*
Catherine A. Kachurik, *Secretary*

AMP Incorporated	Patrick E. Lannan
	C. Brill *(Alt)*
American Bankers Association	Andrew Ernst
	Chris Crawford *(Alt)*
American Express Co.	R.S. Newman
	R.G. Wilson *(Alt)*
American Library Association	Paul Peters
American Nuclear Society	Geraldine C. Main
	D.R. Vondy *(Alt)*
Association for Computer Machinery	J.A.N. Lee
	Pat Skelly *(Alt)*
Association of American Railroads	R.A. Petrash
Association of Computer Users	Hillel Segal
	Thomas Kurihara *(Alt)*
Burroughs Corporation	Ira R. Purchis
	Jerrold S. Foley *(Alt)*
Control Data Corporation	Charles E. Cooper
	Keith Lucke *(Alt)*
Data General Corporation	Steven W. Weingart
	Anthony M. Goschalk *(Alt)*
Data Processing Management Association	Ardyn E. Dubnow
	Joseph A. Federici *(Alt)*
Digital Equipment Computers Users Society	James Hodges
	John R. Barr *(Alt)*
Digital Equipment Corporation	Lois C. Frampton
	Gary S. Robinson *(Alt)*
GUIDE International	Frank Kirshenbaum
	Leland Milligan *(Alt)*
General Services Administration	William C. Rinehuls
	Donald J. Page *(Alt)*
Harris Corporation	Sam Mathan
	David Abmayr *(Alt)*
Hewlett-Packard	Donald C. Loughry
Honeywell Information Systems	Thomas J. McNamara
	Alan Teubner *(Alt)*
IBM Corporation	Mary Anne Gray
	J.S. Wilson *(Alt)*
IEEE Communications Society	Thomas A. Varetoni

IEEE Computer Society	Robert Poston
	Robert A. Stewart (Alt)
Lawrence Berkeley Laboratory	James A. Baker
	Robert J. Harvey (Alt)
Life Office Management Association	John I. Burke
	James F. Foley, Jr. (Alt)
3M Company	R.C. Smith
Moore Business Forms	D.H. Oddy
NCR Corporation	Thomas W. Kern
	William E. Synder (Alt)
National Bureau of Standards	Robert E. Rountree
	James H. Burrows (Alt)
National Communications System	Marshall L. Cain
	George W. White (Alt)
Perkin-Elmer Corporation	David Ellis
	David Saunders (Alt)
Prime Computer	Jeffrey C. Flowers
	Winfried A. Burke (Alt)
Professional Secretaries International	Jerome Heitman
	P.E. Pesce (Alt)
Recognition Technology Users Association	Herbert F. Schantz
	G.W. Wetzel (Alt)
SHARE, Inc.	Thomas B. Steel
	Daniel Schuster (Alt)
Society of Certified Data Processors	Thomas M. Kurihara
	Ardyn E. Dubnow (Alt)
Sperry Univac	Marvin W. Bass
	Charles D. Card (Alt)
Telephone Group	Henry L. Marchese
	J.A. Owen (Alt)
	Stewart M. Garland (Alt)
Texas Instruments, Inc.	Presley Smith
	Don Caraway (Alt)
Travelers Insurance Companies, Inc.	Joseph T. Brophy
US Department of Defense	William LaPlant
	Harry Pontius (Alt)
Wang Laboratories, Inc.	Carl W. Schwarcz
	Marsha Hayek (Alt)
Xerox Corporation	John L. Wheeler
	Arthur R. Machell (Alt)

The Joint ANSI/X3J9-IEEE Pascal Standards Committee which developed this standard had the following members. [6]

6. There is no question that putting together a standard like this is an enormous task, as indicated by the development effort described in the Foreword and the many other individuals and committees involved.

Carol Sledge, *Chairman* Michael P. Hagerty, *Vice Chairman*
David L. Reese, *Secretary* Joe Cointment, *International Representative*

Michael Alexander	Steven Hobbs	Robert Poon
Jeffrey Allen	Albert A. Hoffman	David L. Presberg
Ed Barkmeyer	Robert Hutchins	William C. Price
W. Ashby Boaz	Rosa C. Hwang	Bruce Ravenel*
A. Windsor Brown	Scott Jameson	David C. Robbins
Jerry R. Brookshire	David Jones	Lynne Rosenthal

Tomas M. Burger	Steen Jurs	Tom Rudkin
David S. Cargo	Mel Kanner	Stephen C. Schwarm
Richard J. Cichelli	John Kaufmann	Rick Shaw
Roger Cox	Leslie Klein	Barry Smith
Jean Danver	Bruce Knobe	Rudeen S. Smith
Debra Deutsch	Dennis Kodimer	Bill Stackhouse
Bob Dietrich	Ronald E. Kole	Marius Troost**
Victor A. Falwarczny	Alan A. Kortesoja	Thomas N. Turba
G.G. Gustafson	Edward Krall	Prescott K. Turner
Thomas Giventer	Robert Lange	Howard Turtle
Hellmut Golde	Rainer McCown	Robert Tuttle
David N. Gray	Jim Miner	Richard C. Vile, Jr.
Paul Gregory	Eugene N. Miya	Larry B. Weber
Charles E. Haynes	Mark Molloy	David Weil
Christopher Henrich	Dennis Nicholson	Thomas R. Wilcox
Steven Hiebert	Mark Overgaard	Thomas Wolfe
Ruth Higgins	Ted C. Park	Harvy Wohlwend
Charles Hill	Donald D. Peckham	Kenneth M. Zemrowski
	David Peercy	

*Past Chairman IEEE Pascal Committee
**Past Chairman X3J9 Committee

Others who contributed to the development of this standard are: A.M. Addyman: Chairman BSI OIS/5 and Convener of ISO/TC97/SC5/Working Group 4 Pascal, and the Members of ISO/TC97/SC5/Working Group 4 Pascal.

Thomas N. Turba and Sperry Univac made major contributions to the publication of this edition by editing the approved draft and supplying typeset copy. Their assistance is acknowledged with gratitude.

IEEE Standards documents are developed within the Technical Committees of the IEEE Societies and the Standards Coordinating Committees of the IEEE Standards Board. Members of the commitees serve voluntarily and without compensation. They are not necessarily members of the Institute. The standards developed within IEEE represent a consensus of the broad expertise on the subject within the Institute as well as those activities outside of IEEE which have expressed an interest in participating in the development of the standard.

Use of an IEEE Standard is wholly voluntary. The existence of an IEEE Standard does not imply that there are no other ways to produce, test, measure, purchase, market, or provide other goods and services related to the scope of the IEEE Standard. Furthermore, the viewpoint expressed at the time a standard is approved and issued is subject to change brought about through developments in the state of the art and comments received from users of the standard. Every IEEE Standard is subjected to review at least once every five years for revision or reaffirmation. When a document is more than five years old, and has not been reaffirmed, it is reasonable to conclude that its contents, although still of some value, do not wholly reflect the present state of the art.[7] Users are cautioned to check to determine that they have the latest edition of any IEEE Standard.

Comments for revision of IEEE Standards are welcome from any interested party, regardless of membership affiliation with IEEE. Suggestions for changes in documents should be in the form of a proposed change of text, together with appropriate supporting comments.

Interpretations: Occasionally questions may arise regarding the meaning of portions of standards as they relate to specific applications. When the need for interpretations is brought to the attention of IEEE, the Institute will initiate action to prepare appropriate responses. Since IEEE Standards represent a consensus of all concerned interests, it is important to ensure that any interpretation has also received the concurrence of a balance of interests. For this reason IEEE and the members of its technical committees are not able to provide an instant response to interpretation requests except in those cases where the matter has previously received formal consideration.

Comments on standards and requests for interpretations should be addressed to:

Secretary, IEEE Standards Board
345 East 47th Street
New York, NY 10017
USA

This standard was derived from the second revision of ISO dp7185 and has been updated to include changes to the third revision of ISO dp7185 and responses to public comments on the first draft of ANSI/IEEE 770 X3.97-1983.

[7]. There is already a serious effort to conform to standard Pascal, especially among producers of major compilers. Much of this effort is for the full ISO version with conformant arrays. For implementations on small computers, it is probably fair to say that the Pascal standard will set more of a goal than a reality.

LANGUAGE SPECIFICATION

1. SCOPE

1.1 This standard specifies the semantics and syntax of the computer programming language Pascal by specifying requirements for a processor and for a conforming program.

1.2 This standard does not specify: [8]

(a) The size or complexity of a program and its data that will exceed the capacity of any specific data processing system or the capacity of a particular processor, nor the actions to be taken when the corresponding limits are exceeded;

(b) the minimal requirements of a data processing system that is capable of supporting an implementation of a processor for Pascal;

(c) the method of activating the program-block or the set of commands used to control the environment in which a Pascal program is transformed and executed;

(d) the mechanism by which programs written in Pascal are transformed for use by a data processing system;

(e) the method for reporting errors or warnings;

(f) the typographical representation of a program published for human reading.

[8] The standard makes a conscious effort not to make any statements regarding the implementation of Pascal or its programming environment.

2. REFERENCE

ISO 646 : The 7-bit coded character set for information processing interchange.

3. DEFINITIONS

For the purposes of this standard, the following definitions apply.

NOTE. To draw attention to language concepts, some terms are printed in italics on their first mention in this standard.

9. An "error" here refers to execution errors that may or may not be reported at runtime. For instance, division by zero is considered an "error" (see Section 6.7.2.2) and selecting a case index that does not correspond to one of the alternatives in case statement is considered an "error" (see Section 6.8.3.5). The fact that such "errors" may go undetected leaves the implementation room for judgment as well as loopholes.

3.1 ERROR. A violation by a program of the requirements of this standard that a processor is permitted to leave undetected. [9]

NOTES
1. If it is possible to construct a program in which the violation or non-violation of this standard requires knowledge of the data read by the program or the implementation definition of implementation-defined features, then violation of that requirement is classified as an *error*. Processors may report on such violations of the requirement without such knowledge, but there always remain some cases that require execution or simulated execution, or proof procedures with the required knowledge. Requirements that can be verified without such knowledge are not classified as errors.
2. Processors should attempt the detection of as many errors as possible, and to as complete a degree as possible. Permission to omit detection is provided for implementations in which the detection would be an excessive burden.

10. Extensions must form a superset of standard Pascal. That is, an extended Pascal must still accept all programs conforming to the standard. The exception about identifiers allows extended versions to add new keywords, which prohibit their use as identifiers.

3.2 EXTENSION. A modification to Section 6 of the requirements of this standard that does not invalidate any program complying with this standard, as defined by 5.2, except by prohibiting the use of one or more particular spellings of identifiers. [10]

3.3 IMPLEMENTATION-DEFINED. Possibly differing between processors, but defined for any particular processor.

3.4 IMPLEMENTATION-DEPENDENT. Possibly differing between processors and not necessarily defined for any particular processor.

11. I depart here from the Pascal standard by using a variant of the notation given in the ISO document. This variant (see H. Ledgard, "A Human Engineered Variant of BNF", SIGPLAN Notices, Volume 15, Number 10, October 1980, pages 57-62) goes as follows:

(a) Category names (meta-identifiers) are written in lower-case.

(b) Program symbols (terminal symbols) are written in a special program type face.

(c) Square brackets enclose optional items. When square brackets are themselves meant to be program symbols, the brackets are enclosed by quotation marks.

(d) Sequences of items are denoted by placing "..." after a category name or the closing bracket of an optional item.

In the ISO document, quotes are used to enclose all program symbols and braces are used to enclose sequences. The hope here is to produce more readable syntax equations.

3.5 PROCESSOR. A system or mechanism that accepts a program as input, prepares it for execution, and executes the process so defined with data to produce results.

NOTE. A processor may consist of an interpreter, a compiler and run-time system, or other mechanism, together with an associated host computing machine and operating system, or other mechanism for achieving the same effect. A compiler in itself, for example, does not constitute a processor.

4. DEFINITIONAL CONVENTIONS

The metalanguage used in this standard to specify the syntax of the constructs is based on Backus-Naur Form. The notation has been modified from the original to permit greater convenience of description and to allow for iterative productions to replace recursive ones. Table 1 lists the meanings of the various metasymbols. [11] Further specification of the constructs is given by prose and, in some cases, by equivalent program fragments. Any identifier that is defined in Section 6 as a required identifier shall denote the corresponding required entity by its occurrence in such a program fragment. In all other respects, any such program fragment is bound by any pertinent requirement of this standard.

TABLE 1
Metalanguage Symbols

Metasymbol	Meaning
=	shall be defined to be
|	alternatively
x	an instance of x
x...	1 or more instances of x
[x]	0 or 1 instance of x
[x]...	0 or more instances of x
xyz	the terminal symbol xyz
meta-identifier	a non-terminal symbol

A meta-identifier shall be a sequence of letters and hyphens beginning with a letter.

A sequence of terminal and non-terminal symbols in a production implies the concatenation of the text that they ultimately represent. Within 6.1 this concatenation is direct; no characters shall intervene. In all other parts of this standard the concatenation is in accordance with the rules set out in 6.1.

The characters required to form Pascal programs shall be those implicitly required to form the tokens and separators defined in 6.1.

Use of the words *of, in, containing* and *closest-containing* when expressing a relationship between terminal or non-terminal symbols shall have the following meanings.

the x *of* a y: refers to the x occurring directly in a production defining y.

the x *in* a y: is synonymous with 'the x *of* a y'.

a y *containing* an x: refers to any y from which an x is directly or indirectly derived.

the y closest-containing an x: that y which contains an x but does not contain another y *containing* that x.

12. The words "of", "in", "containing", and "closest-containing" are used throughout the standard. They occur in phrases like "an identifier *in* the identifier list *of* a value-parameter-specification" and "a block *closest-containing* a label-declaration-part." The usage of these words follows conventional English usage. However, the recursive use of these words occasionally requires intense mental effort to follow the meaning.

13. This means that if new features are introduced, a processor may not prohibit or restrict the use of existing features. For instance, consider

```
BIND (DATAFILE, DEVICE4)
```

where BIND is a non-standard procedure associating a file with an i-o device. The processor may not require that all files be bound, but may do so for external files.

14. The meaning here is that all the clauses in the standard like "the case-list-elements of a case-statement shall be distinct" (Section 6.8.3.5) or "after a for-statement is executed the control-variable shall be undefined" (Section 6.8.3.9) shall be enforced by a complying processor. Notice that the word "error" is reserved in the standard for a class of execution errors that may be difficult for some implementations to detect, and hence their detection is optional.

15. This means that extensions are allowed, but must be described separately.

These syntactic conventions [12] are used in Section 6 to specify certain syntactic requirements and also the contexts within which certain semantic specifications apply.

5. COMPLIANCE

5.1 PROCESSORS. A processor complying with the requirements of this standard shall:

(a) accept all the features of the language specified in Section 6 with the meanings defined in Section 6;

(b) (This section intentionally left blank to preserve numbering with ISO dp7185).

(c) not require the inclusion of substitute or additional language elements [13] in a program in order to accomplish a feature of the language that is specified in Section 6;

(d) be accompanied by a document that provides a definition of all implementation-defined features;

(e) be able to determine whether or not a program violates any requirement of this standard, where such a violation is not designated an error, and report the result of this determination to the user of the processor; [14] in the case where the processor does not examine the whole program, the user shall be notified that the determination is incomplete whenever no violations have been detected in the program text examined;

(f) treat each violation that is designated an error in at least one of the following ways:

(1) there shall be a statement in an accompanying document that the error is not reported;
(2) the processor shall report during preparation of the program for execution that an occurrence of that error was possible;
(3) the processor shall report the error during preparation of the program for execution;
(4) the processor shall report the error during execution of the program, and terminate execution of the program;
and if any violations that are designated as errors are treated in the manner described in 5.1(f)(1), then a note referencing each such treatment shall appear in a separate section of the accompanying document;

(g) be accompanied by a document that separately describes any features accepted by the processor that are prohibited or not specified in Section 6; such extensions shall be described as being 'extensions to Pascal as specified by ANSI/IEEE 770 X3.97-1983'; [15]

(h) be able to process in a manner similar to that specified for errors any use of any such extension;

(i) be able to process in a manner similar to that specified for errors any use of an implementation-dependent feature.

NOTES
1. The phrase 'be able to' is used in 5.1 to permit the implementation of a switch with which the user may control the reporting.
2. In cases where the compilation is aborted due to some limitation of tables, etc., an incomplete determination of the kind 'No violations were detected, but the examination is incomplete.' will satisfy the requirements of Section 5.1(e). In a similar manner, an interpretive or direct execution processor may report an incomplete determination for a program of which all aspects have not been examined.

A processor that purports to comply, wholly or partially, with the requirements of this standard shall do so only in the following terms. A *compliance statement* shall be produced by the processor as a consequence of using the processor, or shall be included in accompanying documentation. If the processor complies in all respects with the requirements of this standard the compliance statement shall be:

> *<This processor>* complies with the requirements of ANSI/IEEE 770 X3.97-1983.

If the processor complies with some but not all of the requirements of this standard then it shall not use the above statement, but shall instead use the following compliance statement:

> *<This processor>* complies with the requirements of ANSI/IEEE 770 X3.97-1983,
> with the following exceptions:
> > *<followed by a reference to, or a complete list of, the requirements of the standard with which the processor does not comply>*. [16]

16. This is a neat regulation. Partial implementations of the standard are allowed only if the exceptions are really spelled out.

In both cases the text *<This processor>* shall be replaced by an unambiguous name identifying the processor.

NOTE. Processors that do not comply fully with the requirements of the standard are not required to give full details of their failures to comply in the compliance statement; a brief reference to accompanying documentation that contains a complete list in sufficient detail to identify the defects is sufficient.

5.2 PROGRAMS. A program complying with the requirements of this standard shall:

(a) use only those features of the language specified in Section 6,

(b) not rely on any particular interpretation of implementation-dependent features.

17. There is a subtle distinction in this section in that a program may rely on implementation-*defined* features (note (1)) but shall not rely on any implementation-*dependent* feature (paragraph (b)). Consider the fragment:

```
READ (CH);
{ -- test if CH is a digit }
if  (CH >= ORD('0'))
and (CH <= ORD('9'))
then
   DIGIT := ORD(CH) - ORD('0')
```

This is an acceptable reliance on an implementation-defined feature. However, consider

```
if (INDEX <= MAX)
and (A[INDEX] = HITVALUE)
then ...
```

A program may not rely on a left-to-right evaluation of boolean expressions to avoid exceeding the bounds of the array A.

18. For instance, the exact results of arithmetic on real numbers may give different results on different processors. In the given example program, the value of MAXINT is implementation-defined.

19. The Pascal standard is almost entirely given in Section 6. Sections 1 through 5 discuss some general considerations and are short. Section 6 is the language itself. This gives rise to an unpleasant preponderance of section numbers and cross-references beginning with 6, with nesting to numbers like 6.4.2.3 and 6.9.3.4.1. This stems from ISO regulations.

20. Upper and lower case letters are considered equivalent. Thus the identifiers

```
COUNTER
Counter
counter
```

are all considered as the same.

NOTES
1. A program that complies with the requirements of this standard may rely on particular implementation-defined values or features. [17]
2. The requirements for compliant programs and compliant processors do not require that the results produced by a compliant program are always the same when processed by a compliant processor. [18] They may be, or they may differ, depending on the program. A simple program to illustrate this is:

```
program X(OUTPUT);
begin
    WRITELN(MAXINT)
end.
```

6. REQUIREMENTS

6.1 LEXICAL TOKENS

NOTE. The syntax given in this subsection (6.1) describes the formation of lexical tokens from characters and the separation of these tokens, and therefore does not adhere to the same rules as the syntax in the rest of this standard.

6.1.1 *General.* [19] The lexical tokens used to construct Pascal programs shall be classified into special-symbols, identifiers, directives, unsigned-numbers, labels and character-strings. The representation of any letter (upper-case or lower-case, differences of font, etc.) occurring anywhere outside of a character-string (see 6.1.7) shall be insignificant [20] in that occurrence to the meaning of the program.

```
letter = A | B | C | D | E | F | G | H | I | J | K | L | M
       | N | O | P | Q | R | S | T | U | V | W | X | Y | Z

digit  = 0 | 1 | 2 | 3 | 4 | 5 | 6 | 7 | 8 | 9
```

6.1.2 *Special-Symbols.* The special-symbols are tokens having special meanings and shall be used to delimit the syntactic units of the language.

```
special-symbol = + | - | * | / | = | < | > | [ | ]
               | . | , | : | ; | ↑ | ( | ) | <>
               | <= | >= | := | .. | word-symbol

word-symbol    = and | array | begin | case | const | div | do
               | downto | else | end | file | for | function
               | goto | if | in | label | mod | nil | not | of
               | or | packed | procedure | program | record
               | repeat | set | then | to | type | until | var
               | while | with
```

6.1.3 *Identifiers.* Identifiers may be of any length. All characters of an identifier shall be significant in distinguishing between identifiers. No identifier shall have the same spelling as any word-symbol. Identifiers that are specified to be *required* shall have special significance (see 6.2.2.10 and 6.10).[21]

    identifier = letter [letter | digit]...

Examples:
    X
    TIME
    READINTEGER
    WG4
    ALTERHEATSETTING
    InquireWorkstationTransformation
    InquireWorkstationIndentification

6.1.4 *Directives.* A directive[22] shall occur only in a procedure-declaration or function-declaration. The directive FORWARD shall be the only required directive (see 6.6.1 and 6.6.2). No directive shall have the same spelling as any word-symbol.

    directive = letter [letter | digit]...

NOTE. Many processors provide, as an extension, the directive EXTERNAL, which is used to specify that the procedure-block or function-block corresponding to that procedure-heading or function-heading is external to the program-block. Usually it is in a library in a form to be input to, or that has been produced by, the processor.

6.1.5 *Numbers.* An unsigned-integer shall denote in decimal notation a value of integer-type (see 6.4.2.2). An unsigned-real shall denote in decimal notation a value of real-type (see 6.4.2.2). The letter 'E' preceding a scale factor shall mean *times ten to the power of.* The value denoted by an unsigned-integer shall be in the closed interval 0 to MAXINT (see 6.4.2.2 and 6.7.2.2).

signed-number	=	signed-integer | signed-real
signed-real	=	[sign] unsigned-real
signed-integer	=	[sign] unsigned-integer
unsigned-number	=	unsigned-integer | unsigned-real
sign	=	+ | −
unsigned-real	=	unsigned-integer . fractional-part [E scale-factor]
	|	unsigned-integer E scale-factor
unsigned-integer	=	digit-sequence
fractional-part	=	digit-sequence
scale-factor	=	signed-integer
digit-sequence	=	digit [digit]...

Examples:[23]
    1E10
    1
    +100

21. Because of Section 6.1.8, there is a practical limit on the length of identifiers, that they must fit on a line.

On some systems, however, there is no real limit to the length of a line, and this requirement might be kept. In any case, implementations cannot limit identifiers to eight or ten characters, a common restriction in the past.

No identifier can be a word-symbol, which means the word-symbols are, in effect, reserved keywords. The required identifiers like INTEGER and READ are not reserved and can be redeclared with a new meaning in a program.

22. Aside from the directive FORWARD, directives may be viewed as instructions to the system implementing Pascal, for example.

    procedure GETEXPRESSION (INFILE: TEXT); FORWARD;
      { -- The body of GETEXPRESSION appears later }

    procedure SETPROTOCOLS; EXTERNAL;
      { -- The procedure is compiled externally }

    procedure PLOTPOINT (X, Y: REAL); FORTRAN;
      { -- The procedure is in the Fortran library }

FORWARD is not considered as a keyword or as a required identifier.

23. A real number must have a decimal point or a scale factor, or both. A real number must also have an integer part. Thus the numbers

    .15 3000. E+10

are not allowed.

```
-0.1
5E-3
87.35e+8
```

6.1.6 *Labels.* Labels shall be digit-sequences and shall be distinguished by their apparent integral values and shall be in the closed interval 0 to 9999.

> label = digit-sequence

6.1.7 *Character-Strings.* A character-string containing a single string-element shall denote a value of the required char-type (see 6.4.2.2). A character-string containing more than one string-element shall denote a value of a string-type (see 6.4.3.2) with the same number of components as the character-string contains string-elements. There shall be an implementation-defined one-to-one correspondence between the set of alternatives from which string-elements are drawn and a subset of the values of the required char-type. The occurrence of a string-element in a character-string shall denote the occurrence of the corresponding value of char-type. [24]

24. Thus 'A' denotes a character value and 'AA' denotes a string value. Notice that a null string is not permitted.

character-string	=	' string-element [string-element]... '
string-element	=	apostrophe-image | string-character
apostrophe-image	=	''
string-character	=	one-of-a-set-of-implementation-defined-characters

NOTE. Conventionally, the apostrophe-image is regarded as a substitute for the apostrophe character, which cannot be a string-character.

Examples
```
'A'
'.'
''''
'Pascal'
'THIS IS A STRING'
```

6.1.8 *Token Separators.* The construct

> { any-sequence-of-characters-and-separations-of-lines-not-containing-right-brace }

shall be a comment if the { does not occur within a character-string or within a comment. The substitution of a space for a comment shall not alter the meaning of a program. [25]

25. The standard says that

```
'A { comment } in a string'
```

is a string whose embedded comment cannot be replaced by a space. Implementations must treat the braces as normal string characters. Nested comments are not allowed, which means code containing comments cannot be blocked out as a comment.

Comments, spaces (except in character-strings), and the separation of consecutive lines shall be considered to be token separators. Zero or more token separators may occur between any two consecutive tokens, or before the first token of a program text. There shall be at least one separator between any pair of consecutive tokens made up of identifiers, word-symbols, labels or unsigned-numbers. No separators shall occur within tokens.[26]

6.1.9 Lexical Alternatives.

The representation for lexical tokens and separators given in 6.1.1 to 6.1.8 shall constitute a *reference representation* for these tokens and separators. The reference representation shall be used for program interchange.

To facilitate the use of Pascal on processors that do not support the reference representation, the following alternatives have been defined. All processors that have the required characters in their character set shall provide both the reference representations and the alternative representations, and the corresponding tokens or separators shall not be distinguished.

The alternative representations for the tokens shall be:

Reference token	Alternative token
↑	@
[	(.
]	.)

NOTE. The "hat" character that appears in some national variants of ISO 646 is regarded as identical to the character ↑. In this standard, the character ↑ has been used because of its greater visibility.

The alternative forms of comment shall be all forms of comment where one or both of the following substitutions are made:

Delimiting character	Alternative delimiting pair of characters
{	(*
}	*)

NOTES
1. A comment may thus commence with { and end with *), or commence with (* and end with }.
2. If the sequence (*) occurs in a comment, it is equivalent to {} and marks the end of the comment, because the substitution is only for a delimiting character.
3. See also 1.2(f).

6.2 BLOCKS, SCOPE AND ACTIVATIONS

6.2.1 Block

A block closest-containing a label-declaration-part in which a label occurs shall closest-contain exactly one statement in which that label occurs.[27] The occurrence of a label in the label-declaration-part of a block shall be its defining point as a label for the region that is the block.

26. Except *within* tokens, spaces may be inserted freely within a Pascal program. This means that

```
goto 4 4
A : = B
(HIT RATE * 4)
```

are not allowed.

Because a comment can be treated as a space, comments can occur at the beginning of a program, as in

```
{ -- Comments can go here }
program VERYSHORT;
begin
    { -- do nothing }
end.
{ -- Comments can also go here }
{ -- in some implementations }
```

As for comments after the end of a program, the standard does not explicitly allow them although some implementations do.

27. This means that if a label is declared it must be used as the label of some statement in the same block, but not in a nested block. Goto's referring to the label can, however, occur in a nested block (see 6.8.1).

28. Notice that all declarative items are optional and thus the entire declaration part can be empty.

```
block 28  =  label-declaration-part
             constant-definition-part
             type-definition-part
             variable-declaration-part
             procedure-and-function-declaration-part
             statement-part
```

label-declaration-?part	=	[label label [, label]... ;]
constant-definition-part	=	[const constant-definition ; [constant-definition ;]...]
type-definition-part	=	[type type-definition ; [type-definition ;]...]
variable-declaration-part	=	[var variable-declaration ; [variable-declaration ;]...]
procedure-and-function-declaration-part	=	[procedure-or-function-declaration ;]...
procedure-or-function-declaration	=	procedure-declaration | function-declaration

This statement-part shall specify the algorithmic actions to be executed upon an activation of the block.

```
statement-part = compound-statement
```

6.2.2 Scope

6.2.2.1 Each identifier or label contained by the program-block shall have a defining-point.

6.2.2.2 Each defining-point shall have a region that is a part of the program text, and a scope that is a part or all of that region. **29**

29. A "defining-point" is, in essence, the place where an identifier is associated with its meaning. Normally, say for variables and types, this is where the identifier is explicitly declared. The concept is extended to include enumerated identifiers, field identifiers in a record structure, formal parameters, record variables in a with statement, and the required identifiers.

A "scope" is the portion of program text where an identifier and its defined meaning are linked. Mainly because of nesting of functions and procedures, an identifier can be linked with different meanings. Account must also be made for the field identifiers of a record structure and nested record structures. The concept of "region" is almost a synonym for scope but does not take account of nesting. When there is nesting, the innermost definition of the identifier is used.

6.2.2.3 The region of each defining-point is defined elsewhere (see 6.2.1, 6.2.2.10, 6.3, 6.4.1, 6.4.2.3, 6.4.3.3, 6.5.1, 6.5.3.3, 6.6.1, 6.6.2, 6.6.3.1, 6.8.3.10, 6.10).

6.2.2.4 The scope of each defining-point shall be its region (including all regions enclosed by that region) subject to 6.2.2.5 and 6.2.2.6.

6.2.2.5 When an identifier or label has a defining-point for region A and another identifier or label having the same spelling has a defining-point for some region B enclosed by A, then region B and all regions enclosed by B shall be excluded from the scope of the defining-point for region A.

6.2.2.6 The region that is the field-specifier of a field-designator shall be excluded from the enclosing scopes.

6.2.2.7 When an identifier or label has a defining-point for a region, another identifier or label with the same spelling shall not have a defining point for that region. [30]

6.2.2.8 Within the scope of a defining-point of an identifier or label, each occurrence of an identifier or label having the same spelling as the identifier or label of the defining-point shall be designated an applied occurrence of the identifier or label of the defining-point, except for an occurrence that constituted the defining-point of that identifier or label; such an occurrence shall be designated a defining occurrence. No occurrence outside that scope shall be an applied occurrence.

NOTE. Within the scope of a defining-point of an identifier or label, there are no applied occurrences of an identifier or label that cannot be distinguished from it and have a defining-point for a region enclosing that scope.

6.2.2.9 The defining-point of an identifier or label shall precede all applied occurrences of that identifier or label contained by the program-block with one exception, namely that an identifier may have an applied occurrence in the type-identifier of the domain-type of any new-pointer-types contained by the type-definition-part that contains the defining-point of the type-identifier. [31]

6.2.2.10 Identifiers that denote required constants, types, procedures and functions shall be used as if their defining-points have a region enclosing the program [32] (see 6.1.3, 6.3, 6.4.1 and 6.6.4.1).

NOTE. The required identifiers INPUT and OUTPUT are not included, since these denote variables.

6.2.2.11 Whatever an identifier or label denotes at its defining-point shall be denoted at all applied occurrences of that identifier or label.

NOTE. Within syntax definitions, an applied occurrence of an identifier is qualified, e.g. type-identifier, whereas a use that constitutes a defining-point is not qualified.

6.2.3 *Activations*

6.2.3.1 A procedure-identifier or function-identifier having a defining-point for a region that is a block within the procedure-and-function-declaration-part of that block shall be designated *local* to that block.

6.2.3.2 The activation of a block shall contain:

30. Except for nesting it is incorrect to redefine an identifier in the same declarative part. Thus

```
const
    PI = 3.14;
var
    PI: REAL;
```

and

```
type
    PENPOSITION = (UP, DOWN);
var
    UP: REAL;
```

are incorrect. Record structures are a special case (see Section 6.4.3.3), and the declarations

```
type
    COORDINATE = record
                    X: REAL;
                    Y: REAL
                  end;
    LINE = record
             POINT1: COORDINATE;
             POINT2: COORDINATE
           end;
var
    X: REAL;
    C: COORDINATE;
    L: LINE;
```

are allowed.

In the corresponding statement part we may have the following

```
X         { -- the real variable X }
C.X       { -- the X component of the record C }
L.POINT1.X { -- the X component of L.POINT1 }
```

31. This means that the definition of an identifier must precede its use. The exception is needed to handle pointer types as in

```
type
    PERSON = ↑INFO; { -- INFO is defined below }
    INFO   = record
               NAME:      STRING;
               SSNUM:     INTEGER;
               NEXTOFKIN: PERSON
             end;
```

32. The required identifiers like INTEGER (the predefined type) or READ (the predefined procedure) are treated as if they are defined just outside a program. This means that these identifiers can be redefined in a program. Thus something horrible like

```
var
   INTEGER, READ, TRUE: REAL;
```

is allowed.

33. It is this that essentially makes recursion work. For instance in

```
procedure P;
   LOCALVAR: INTEGER;
begin
   ...
   P;  { -- one activation }
   ...
   P;  { -- another }
   ...
end;
```

the two calls to P may produce different results. Each will have its own copy of LOCALVAR. See example (3) in Section 6.10.

(a) for the statement-part of the block, an algorithm, the completion of which shall terminate the activation (see also 6.8.2.4);

(b) for each label in a statement having a defining-point in the label-declaration-part of the block, a program-point in the algorithm of the activation at that statement;

(c) for each variable-identifier having a defining-point for the region that is the block, a variable possessing the type associated with the variable-identifier;

(d) for each procedure-identifier local to the block, a procedure with the procedure-block corresponding to the procedure-identifier, and the formal parameters of that procedure-block;

(e) for each function-identifier local to the block, a function with the function-block corresponding to, and the result type associated with, the function-identifier, and the formal parameters of that function-block;

(f) if the block is a function-block, a result possessing the associated result type.

NOTE. Each activation contains its own algorithm, set of program-points, set of variables, set of procedures, and set of functions, distinct from every other activation. **33**

6.2.3.3 The activation of a procedure or function shall be the activation of the block of its procedure-block or function-block, respectively, and shall be designated as within:

(a) the activation containing the procedure or function; and
(b) all activations that that containing activation is within.

NOTE. An activation of a block B can only be within activations of blocks containing B. Thus an activation is not within another activation of the same block.

Within an activation, an applied occurrence of a label or variable-identifier, or of a procedure-identifier or function-identifier local to the block of the activation, shall denote the corresponding program-point, variable, procedure, or function, respectively, of that activation; except that the function-identifier of an assignment-statement shall, within an activation of the function denoted by that function-identifier, denote the result of that activation.

6.2.3.4 A procedure-statement or function-designator contained in the algorithm of an activation and that specifies the activation of a block shall be designated the activation-point of that activation of the block.

6.2.3.5 All variables contained by an activation, except for those listed as program-parameters, and any result of an activation, shall be totally-undefined at the commencement of that activation. The algorithm, program-points, variables, procedures and functions, if any, shall exist until the termination of the activation.

6.3 CONSTANT-DEFINITIONS.
A constant-definition shall introduce an identifier to denote a value.

constant-definition	=	identifier = constant
constant	=	[sign] unsigned-number
	|	[sign] constant-identifier
	|	character-string
constant-identifier	=	identifier

The occurrence of an identifier in a constant-definition of a constant-definition part of a block shall constitute its defining-point for the region that is the block. The constant in a constant-definition shall not contain an applied occurrence of the identifier in the constant-definition. Each applied occurrence of that identifier shall be a constant-identifier and shall denote the value denoted by the constant of the constant-definition. A constant-identifier in a constant containing an occurrence of a sign shall have been defined to denote a value of real-type or of integer-type. The required constant-identifiers shall be as specified in 6.4.2.2 and 6.7.2.2.[34]

6.4 TYPE-DEFINITIONS

6.4.1 *General.* A type-definition shall introduce an identifier to denote a type. Type shall be an attribute that is possessed by every value and every variable. Each occurrence of a new-type shall denote a type that is distinct from any other new-type.[35]

type-definition	=	identifier = type-denoter
type-denoter	=	type-identifier | new-type
new-type	=	new-ordinal-type
	|	new-structured-type
	|	new-pointer-type

The occurrence of an identifier in a type-definition of a type-definition-part of a block shall constitute its defining-point for the region that is the block. Each applied occurrence of that identifier shall be a type-identifier and shall denote the same type as that which is denoted by the type-denoter of the type-definition. Except for applied occurrences in the domain-type of a new-pointer-type, the type-denoter shall not contain an applied occurrence of the identifier in the type-definition.[36]

Types shall be classified as simple, structured or pointer types. The required type-identifiers and corresponding required types shall be as specified in 6.4.2.2 and 6.4.3.5.

34. Thus we may have

```
const
  PI      = 3.14159;   { -- unsigned number }
  NEGPI   = -PI;        { -- signed number }
  HEADER  = 'PROFITS';  { -- character string }
  DAY1    = MONDAY;     { -- enumerated value }
  COPY    = HEADER;     { -- declared constant }
  SUCCESS = TRUE;       { -- required constant }
```

but not

```
const
  TWOPI = 2*PI;   { -- no multiplication }
  VALUE1 = A[1];  { -- not a constant }
```

35. Thus in

```
type
  GRADES = array [1..10] of INTEGER;
  SCORES = array [1..10] of INTEGER;
```

two distinct types names GRADES and SCORES, are defined but in

```
type
  DATA   = array [1..10] of INTEGER;
  GRADES = DATA;
  SCORES = DATA;
```

GRADES and SCORES are considered as different identifiers denoting the same type. In the variable declarations

```
A, B: array [1..10] of INTEGER;
```

A and B have the same type, but in

```
C: array [1..10] of INTEGER;
D: array [1..10] of INTEGER;
```

C and D have different types. Thus

```
A := B
```

is allowed, but

```
C := D
```

is not.

36. The exception mentioned here allows type definitions like

```
type
   LISTITEM = record
                 VALUE: INTEGER;
                 NEXT:  ↑LISTITEM
              end;
var
   A, B: LISTITEM;
```

37. Pascal considers integers to be in the range –MAXINT to MAXINT. On a 2's complement machine, MAXINT would be $2^{n-1}-1$, but the range of integers would be

$$-2^{n-1} .. 2^{n-1} -1$$

Thus the implementation would support an extra negative value.

38. Thus FALSE < TRUE is true and booleans have ordinal values. Some believe this matter should be undefined, since one can say

```
I := I + ORD(BOOLEANVAR)
```

39. Although characters can have implementation assigned integer values (ordinals), if there are, say, 128 characters, they must be assigned ordinal values from 0 to 127.

simple-type-identifier	=	type-identifier
structured-type-identifier	=	type-identifier
pointer-type-identifier	=	type-identifier
type-identifier	=	identifier

A type-identifier shall be considered as a simple-type-identifier, a structured-type-identifier, or a pointer-type-identifier, according to the type that it denotes.

6.4.2 Simple-Types

6.4.2.1 *General.* A simple-type shall determine an ordered set of values. The values of each ordinal-type shall have integer ordinal numbers. An ordinal-type identifier shall denote an ordinal-type.

simple-type	=	ordinal-type	real-type-identifier
ordinal-type	=	new-ordinal-type	ordinal-type-identifier
new-ordinal-type	=	enumerated-type	subrange-type
ordinal-type-identifier	=	type-identifier
real-type-identifier	=	type-identifier

6.4.2.2 *Required Simple-Types.* The following types shall exist:

(a) *integer-type.* The required ordinal-type-identifier INTEGER shall denote the integer-type. The values shall be a subset of the whole numbers, denoted as specified in 6.1.5 by signed-integer (see also 6.7.2.2). [37] The ordinal number of a value of integer-type shall be the value itself.

(b) *real-type.* The required real-type-identifier REAL shall denote the real-type. The values shall be an implementation-defined subset of the real numbers denoted as specified in 6.1.5 by signed-real.

(c) *Boolean-type.* The required ordinal-type-identifier BOOLEAN shall denote the Boolean-type. The values shall be the enumeration of truth values denoted by the required constant-identifiers FALSE and TRUE, such that FALSE is the predecessor of TRUE. The ordinal numbers of the truth values denoted by FALSE and TRUE shall be the integer values 0 and 1 respectively. [38]

(d) *char-type.* The required ordinal-type-identifier CHAR shall denote the char-type. The values shall be the enumeration of a set of implementation-defined characters, some possibly without graphic representations. The ordinal numbers of the character values shall be values of integer-type, that are implementation-defined, and that are determined by mapping the character values on to consecutive non-negative integer values starting at zero. [39] The mapping shall be order preserving. The following relations shall hold.

(1) The subset of character values representing the digits 0 to 9 shall be numerically ordered and contiguous.

(2) The subset of character values representing the upper-case letters A to Z, if available, shall be alphabetically ordered but not necessarily contiguous.

(3) The subset of character values representing the lower-case letters a to if available, shall be alphabetically ordered but not necessarily contiguous.[40]

(4) The ordering relationship between any two character values shall be the same as between their ordinal numbers.

NOTE. Operators applicable to the required simple-types are specified in 6.7.2.

6.4.2.3 *Enumerated-Types.*

An enumerated-type shall determine an ordered set of values by enumeration of the identifiers that denote those values. The ordering of these values shall be determined by the sequence in which their identifiers are enumerated, i.e. if x precedes y then x is less than y. The ordinal number of a value that is of an enumerated-type shall be determined by mapping all the values of the type on to consecutive non-negative values of integer-type starting from zero. The mapping shall be order preserving.

```
enumerated-type = ( identifier-list )
identifier-list = identifier [ , identifier ]...
```

The occurrence of an identifier in the identifier-list of an enumerated-type shall constitute its defining-point as a constant-identifier for the region that is the block closest-containing the enumerated-type.[41]

Examples:
```
(RED, YELLOW, GREEN, BLUE, TARTAN)
(CLUB, DIAMOND, HEART, SPADE)
(MARRIED, DIVORCED, WIDOWED, SINGLE)
(SCANNING, FOUND, NOTPRESENT)
(Busy, InterruptEnable, ParityError, OutOfPaper, LineBreak)
```

6.4.2.4 *Subrange-Types.*

A subrange-type shall include identification of the smallest and the largest value in the subrange. The first constant of a subrange-type shall specify the smallest value, and this shall be less than or equal to the largest value which shall be specified by the other constant of the subrange-type. Both constants shall be of the same ordinal-type, and that ordinal-type shall be designated the host type of the subrange-type.[42]

```
subrange-type = constant .. constant
```

Examples
```
1..100
```

40. This allows EBCDIC characters where letters do not have contiguous ordinal values.

41. Because of the scope rules, this means that an identifier cannot occur in more than one enumerated type. Thus

```
type
   COLOR = (RED, YELLOW, GREEN, BLUE);
   SURNAME = (SMITH, JONES, GREEN);
```

is not allowed. However, if the definition of SURNAME appeared instead in a nested procedure, the definition would be allowed. Any reference to GREEN in the nested procedure would refer to the surname and not the color.

42. First note that (see section 6.4.1) that a subrange defines a type different from its host type. This point of view, however, is a bit deceiving. Because of the definitions of type compatibility (Section 6.4.5) and assignment compatibility (Section 6.4.6) a variable of a subrange type or its host type can (aside from range checks) frequently be used interchangeably. Furthermore, arithmetic and relational operators make no distinction between a variable of a subrange or host type. The type difference really comes into play with variable parameters (see 6.6.3.3), and function and procedure parameters (see 6.6.3.6), where a subrange type and the host type are not interchangeable.

As a minor point, notice that the subranges

```
1.0..100.0   { -- real values }
1..0         { -- non-overlapping range }
```

are not allowed.

```
-10..+10
RED..GREEN
'0'..'9'
```

6.4.3 Structured-Types

6.4.3.1 *General.* A new-structured-type shall be classified as an array-type, record-type, set-type or file-type according to the unpacked-structured-type closest-contained by the new-structured-type. A component of a value of a structured-type shall be a value.

structured-type	=	new-structured-type
		structured-type-identifier
new-structured-type	=	[packed] unpacked-structured-type
unpacked-structured-type	=	array-type | record-type
		set-type | file-type

The occurrence of the token *packed* in a new-structured-type shall designate the type denoted thereby as packed. The designation of a structured-type as packed shall indicate to the processor that data-storage of values should be economized, even if this causes operations on, or accesses to components of, variables possessing the type to be less efficient in terms of space or time.[43]

The designation of a structured-type as packed shall affect the representation in data-storage of that structured-type only; i.e., if a component is itself structured, the component's representation in data-storage shall be packed only if the type of the component is designated packed.

NOTE. The ways in which the treatment of entities of a type is affected by whether or not the type is designated packed are specified in 6.4.3.2, 6.4.5, 6.6.3.3, 6.6.5.4 and 6.7.1.

6.4.3.2 *Array-Types.* An array-type shall be structured as a mapping from each value specified by its index-type[44] on to a distinct component. Each component shall have the type denoted by the type-denoter of the component-type of the array-type.

array-type = array "[" index-type [, index-type]... "]" of component-type

index-type	=	ordinal-type
component-type	=	type-denoter

Examples:
```
array [1..100] of REAL
array [BOOLEAN] of COLOUR
```

An array-type that specifies a sequence of two or more index-types shall be an abbreviated notation for an array-type specified to have as its index-

43. Packed structures are a matter for the implementation. It is not *required* that anything special be done, and it is possible for the implementation to take no special action.

44. The index type can be any ordinal type. Thus

```
array [1..10] of INTEGER
array [MONDAY..FRIDAY] of INTEGER
array [BOOLEAN] of INTEGER
array ['A'..'Z'] of INTEGER
```

are all acceptable array types.

type the first index-type in the sequence, and to have a component-type that is an array-type specifying the sequence of index-types without the first and specifying the same component-type as the original specification. The component-type thus constructed shall be designated packed if and only if the original array-type is designated packed. The abbreviated form and the full form shall be equivalent.

NOTE. Each of the following two examples thus contains different ways of expressing its array-type.

Example 1:
```
array [BOOLEAN] of array [1..10] of array [SIZE] of REAL
array [BOOLEAN] of array [1..10, SIZE] of REAL
array [BOOLEAN, 1..10, SIZE] of REAL
array [BOOLEAN, 1..10] of array [SIZE] of REAL
```

Example 2:
```
packed array [1..10, 1..8] of BOOLEAN
packed array [1..10] of packed array [1..8] of BOOLEAN
```

Let i denote a value of the index-type; let v[i] denote a value of that component of the array type that corresponds to the value i by the structure of the array-type; let the smallest and largest values specified by the index-type be denoted by m and n; and let $k = (ORD(n) - ORD(m) + 1)$ denote the number of values specified by the index-type; then the values of the array-type shall be the distinct k-tuples of the form

$$(v[m], \dots, v[n])$$

NOTE. A value of an array-type does not therefore exist unless all of its component values are defined. If the component-type has c values, then it follows that the cardinality of the set of values of the array-type is c raised to the power k.

Any type designated packed and denoted by an array-type having as its index-type a denotation of a subrange-type specifying a smallest value of 1 and a largest value of greater than 1, and having as its component-type a denotation of the char-type, shall be designated a *string-type*. [45]

The correspondence of character-strings to values of string-types is obtained by relating the individual string-elements of the character-string, taken in textual order, to the components of the values of the string-type in order of increasing index.

NOTE. The values of a string-type possess additional properties which allow writing them to textfiles (see 6.9.3.6) and define their use with relational-operators (see 6.7.2.5).

6.4.3.3 *Record-Types.* The structure and values of a record-type shall be the structure and values of the field-list of the record-type.

45. Thus

```
packed array [1..10] of CHAR;
```

denotes a string type with 10 characters, but

```
packed array [1..10] of 'A'..'Z'
```

does not.
   Notice that the equivalence rule for packed arrays makes

```
packed aray [1..10,1..10] of CHAR
```

equivalent to

```
packed array [1..10] of
    packed array [1..10] of CHAR
```

not

```
packed array [1..10] of
    array [1..10] of CHAR
```

46. Notice that the last item in the field list of a record structure, for example,

```
record
   A: INTEGER;
   B: INTEGER;  { -- optional semicolon }
end
```

can have a semicolon.

47. Records with an empty field list are allowed. Normally an empty field list will arise in a variant part where one or more variants are empty (see the second example at the end of 6.4.3.3).

48. Because the scope of a field identifier is the "closest containing" record, nested record structures with identical field identifiers like

```
record
   A: record
         A: INTEGER;
         B: INTEGER
      end
   B: INTEGER
end
```

are allowed. Even

```
type A =
   record
      A: INTEGER;
      B: INTEGER
   end;
```

is allowed.

record-type = record
field-list
end

field-list = [fixed-part [; variant-part] [;] [46]]
| [variant-part [;]]

fixed-part = record-section [;
record-section]...

record-section = indentifier-list : type-denoter

variant-part = case variant-selector of
variant [;
variant]...

variant-selector = [tag-field :] tag-type
tag-field = identifier
variant = case-constant-list : (field-list)
tag-type = ordinal-type-identifier

case-constant-list = case-constant [, case-constant]...
case-constant = constant

A field-list that contains neither a fixed-part nor a variant-part shall have no components, shall define a single null value, and shall be designated empty. [47]

The occurrence of an identifier in the identifier-list of a record-section of a fixed-part of a field-list shall constitute its defining-point as a field-identifier for the region that is the record-type closest-containing the field-list, and shall associate the field-identifier with a distinct component, which shall be designated a *field*, of the record-type and of the field-list. That component shall have the type denoted by the type-denoter of the record-section. [48]

The field-list closest-containing a variant-part shall have a distinct component that shall have the values and structures defined by the variant-part.

Let Vi denote the value of the i-th component of a non-empty field-list having m components; then the values of the field-list shall be distinct m-tuples of the form

(V1, V2, ... ,Vm).

NOTE. If the type of the i-th component has Fi values, then the cardinality of the set of values of the field-list shall be (F1 * F2 * ... * Fm).

A tag-type shall denote the type denoted by the ordinal-type-identifier of the tag-type. A case-constant shall denote the value denoted by the constant of the case-constant.

The type of each case-constant in the case-constant-list of a variant of a variant-part shall be compatible with the tag-type of the variant-selector of the variant-part. The values denoted by all case-constants of a type that is required to be compatible with a given tag-type shall be distinct and the set thereof shall be equal to the set of values specified by the tag-type. [49] The values denoted by the case-constants of the case-constant-list of a variant shall be designated as corresponding to the variant.

With each variant-part shall be associated a type designated the selector-type possessed by the variant-part. If the variant-selector of the variant-part contains a tag-field, or if the case-constant-list of each variant of the variant-part contains only one case-constant, then the selector-type shall be denoted by the tag-type, and each variant of the variant-part shall be associated with those values specified by the selector-type denoted by the case-constants of the case-constant-list of the variant. Otherwise, the selector-type possessed by the variant-part shall be a new ordinal-type constructed such that there is exactly one value of the type for each variant of the variant-part, and no others, and each variant shall be associated with a distinct value of that type. [50]

Each variant-part shall have a component that shall be designated the *selector* of the variant-part, and which shall possess the selector-type of the variant-part. If the variant-selector of the variant-part contains a tag-field, then the occurrence of an identifier in the tag-field shall constitute the defining-point of the identifier as a field-identifier for the region that is the record-type closest-containing the variant-part, and shall associate the field-identifier with the selector of the variant-part. The selector shall be designated a field of the record-type if and only if it is associated with a field-identifier.

Each variant of a variant-part shall denote a distinct component of the variant-part; the component shall have the values and structure of the field-list of the variant, and shall be associated with those values specified by the selector-type possessed by the variant-part associated with the variant. The value of the selector of the variant-part shall cause the associated variant and component of the variant-part to be in a state that shall be designated *active*.

The values of a variant-part shall be the distinct pairs

(k, Xk)

where k represents a value of the selector of the variant-part, and Xk is a value of the field-list of the active variant of the variant-part.

NOTES
1. If there are n values specified by the selector-type, and if the field-list of the variant associated with the i-th value has Ti values, then the cardinality of the set of values of the variant-part is $(T1 + T2 + ... + Tn)$. There is no component of a value of a variant-part corresponding to any non-active variant of the variant-part.
2. Restrictions placed on the use of fields of a record-variable pertaining to variant-parts are specified in 6.5.3.3, and 6.6.3.3 and 6.6.5.3.

49. All values of the tag type must be accounted for in the case constant list of possible variants.

50. Consider the following sketch of a variant part

```
case AGE of
  1, 2, 3: ( ... );
  4, 5:    ( ... );
  6:       ( ... )
```

where

```
type
  AGE = 1..6;
```

Here there are three (not six) variants.

Examples:

```
record
    YEAR:  0..2000;
    MONTH: 1..12;
    DAY:   1..31
end

record
    NAME:      STRING;
    FIRSTNAME: STRING;
    AGE:       0..99;
    case MARRIED: BOOLEAN of
        TRUE:  (SPOUSESNAME: STRING);
        FALSE: ()
end

record
    X, Y: REAL;
    AREA: REAL;
    case SHAPE of 51
        TRIANGLE:
            (SIDE: REAL;   INCLINATION, ANGLE1, ANGLE2: ANGLE);
        RECTANGLE:
            (SIDE1, SIDE2: REAL;   SKEW: ANGLE);
        CIRCLE:
            (DIAMETER: REAL)
end
```

51. Here SHAPE is a tag type, not a tag field. This is an example of an un-named tag field. The active variant is implicitly set by assignment to one of its components. For instance, if R is a record of the type shown

```
R.SIDE2 := 12.3
```

establishes RECTANGLE as the active variant.

6.4.3.4 *Set-Types.* A set-type shall determine the set of values that is structured as the powerset of the base-type of the set-type. Thus each value of a set-type shall be a set whose members shall be unique values of the base-type.

```
set-type  = set of base-type
base-type = ordinal-type
```

NOTE. Operators applicable to values of set-types are specified in 6.7.2.4.

Examples:
```
set of CHAR
set of (CLUB, DIAMOND, HEART, SPADE)
```

NOTE. If the base-type of a set-type has b values then the cardinality of the set of values is 2 raised to the power b.

For every ordinal-type S, there exists an unpacked set type designated the *unpacked canonical set-of-T type* and there exists a packed set type designated the *packed canonical set-of-T type.* [52] If S is a subrange-type then T is the host type of S; otherwise T is S. Each value of the type set of S is also a value of the unpacked canonical set-of-T type, and each value of the type packed set of S is also a value of the packed canonical set-of-T type.

52. When set types are discussed, there is always mention of a "canonical set-of-T" type. The reason for this is similar to the use of host types of a subrange; when we add two values of an integer subrange, the result is of type integer, not of the subrange type. For sets, a similar reasoning holds. For instance, the set [2, 4, 6] implicitly defines a kind of host type, a set of integers. This is the "canonical" type.

6.4.3.5 File-Types

NOTE. A file-type describes sequences of values of the specified component-type, together with a current position in each sequence and a mode that indicates whether the sequence is being inspected or generated.

```
file-type = file of component-type
```

A type-denoter shall not be permissible as the component-type of a file-type if it denotes either a file-type[53] or a structured-type having any component whose type-denoter is not permissible as the component-type of a file-type.

Examples:
```
file of REAL
file of VECTOR
```

A file-type shall define implicitly a type designated a *sequence-type* having exactly those values, which shall be designated *sequences,* defined by the following five rules in items (a) to (e).[54]

NOTE. The notation x • y represents the concatenation of sequences x and y. The explicit representation of sequences (e.g. S(c)), of concatenation of sequences, of the first, last and rest selectors, and of sequence equality is not part of the Pascal language. These notations are used to define file values, below, and the required file operations in 6.6.5.2 and 6.6.6.5.

(a) S() shall be a value of the sequence-type S, and shall be designated the *empty sequence.* The empty sequence shall have no components.

(b) Let c be a value of the specified component-type, and let x be a value of the sequence-type S; then S(c) shall be a sequence of type S, consisting of the single component value c, and both S(c) • x and x • S(c) shall be sequences, distinct from S(), of type S.

(c) Let c, S, and x be as in (b); let y denote the sequence S(c) • x; and let z denote the sequence x • S(c); then the notation y.first shall denote c (i.e., the first component value of y), y.rest shall denote x (i.e., the sequence obtained from y by deleting the first component), and z.last shall denote c (i.e., the last component value of z).

(d) Let x and y each be a non-empty sequence of type S; then x = y shall be true if and only if both (x.first = y.first) and (x.rest = y.rest) are true. If x or y is the empty sequence, then x = y shall be true if and only if both x and y are the empty sequence.

(e) Let x, y, and z be sequences of type S; then x • (y • z) = (x • y) • z, S() • x = x, and x • S() = x shall be true.

A file-type also shall define implicitly a type designated a *mode-type* having exactly two values which are designated *Inspection* and *Generation.*[55]

53. Files containing component files, either directly or indirectly, are not allowed.

54. The rules say

(a) The empty file is a file.

(b) A file containing a single component is a file, and a single component can be appended to a file.

(c) File components are sequentially ordered. There is a first and last component. When the first component is removed, the remaining components comprise the "rest" of the file.

(d) Two files are equal if and only if they have the same number of components and the components themselves are pairwise equal.

(e) The items in a file are appended in sequential order.

55. A file is in one of two states: capable of being read (inspection) or capable of being written (generation). Both activities cannot go on simultaneously.

NOTE. The explicit denotation of the values Inspection and Generation is not part of the Pascal language.

A file-type shall be structured as three components. Two of these components, designated f.L and f.R, shall be of the implicit sequence-type. The third component, designated f.M, shall be of the implicit mode-type.

Let f.L and f.R each be a single value of the sequence-type; let f.M be a single value of the mode-type; then each value of the file-type shall be a distinct triple of the form

(f.L, f.R, f.M)

where f.R shall be the empty sequence if f.M is the value Generation. The value, f, of the file-type shall be designated empty if and only if f.L • f.R is the empty sequence. [56]

56. Intuitively a triple can be interpreted as

(left-part, right-part, read-write-mode)

For files in write-mode, the right part is always considered empty.

NOTE. The two components, f.L and f.R, of a value of the file-type may be considered to represent the single sequence f.L • f.R together with a current position in that sequence. If f.R is non-empty, then f.R.first may be considered the current component as determined by the current position; otherwise, the current position is designated the end-of-file position.

There shall be a file-type that is denoted by the required structured-type-identifier TEXT. The structure of the type denoted by TEXT shall define an additional sequence-type whose values shall be designated *lines*. A line shall be a sequence cs • S(e), where cs is a sequence of components having the char-type, and e represents a special component value, which shall be designated an *end-of-line*, and which shall be indistinguishable from the char value space [57] except by the required function EOLN (see 6.6.6.5) and by the required procedures RESET (see 6.6.5.2), WRITELN (see 6.9.4), and PAGE (see 6.9.5). If *l* is a line then no component of *l* other than *l*.last shall be an end-of-line. These provisions describe the functionality only, and shall not be construed to determine in any way the underlying representation of textfiles; in particular, the relationship, if any, between end-of-line and values of the char-type shall be implementation-dependent.

57. A textfile is a sequence of lines each terminated by an end-of-line marker. When reading the characters of a textfile with, say, GET or READ, an end-of-line marker will be read as a space.

A line-sequence, *ls*, shall be either the empty sequence or the sequence *ls'* where *l* is a line and *ls'* is a line-sequence.

Every value t of the type denoted by TEXT shall satisfy one of the following two rules.

(a) If t.M = Inspection, then t.L • t.R shall be a line-sequence.

(b) If t.M = Generation, then t.L • t.R shall be ls • cs, where *ls* is a line-sequence and cs is a sequence of components possessing the char-type.

58. This is just what one would expect. When generating a file of text, partial lines (those not yet having an end-of-line marker) can occur.

NOTE. In rule (b), cs may be considered, especially if it is non-empty, to be a partial line [58] that is being generated. Such a partial line cannot occur during inspection of a file. Also, cs does not correspond to t.R since t.R is the empty sequence if t.M = Generation.

A variable that possesses the type denoted by the required structured-type-identifier TEXT shall be designated a *textfile*.

NOTE. All required procedures and functions applicable to a variable of type *file of CHAR* are applicable to textfiles. Additional required procedures and functions, applicable only to textfiles,[59] are defined in 6.6.6.5 and 6.9.

6.4.4 *Pointer-Types.* The values of a pointer-type shall consist of a single nil-value, and a set of identifying-values each identifying a distinct variable possessing the domain-type of the pointer-type. The set of identifying-values shall be dynamic, in that the variables and the values identifying them may be created and destroyed during the execution of the program. Identifying-values and the variables identified by them shall be created only by the required procedure NEW (see 6.6.5.3).[60]

NOTE. Since the nil-value is not an identifying-value it does not identify a variable.

The token *nil* shall denote the nil-value in all pointer-types.

```
pointer-type        = new-pointer-type  |  pointer-type-identifier

new-pointer-type    = ↑ domain-type
domain-type         = type-identifier
```

NOTE. The token *nil* does not have a single type, but assumes a suitable pointer-type to satisfy the assignment-compatibility rules, or the compatibility rules for operators, if possible.

6.4.5 *Compatible Types.* Types T1 and T2 shall be designated *compatible* if any of the following four statements is true.[61]

(a) T1 and T2 are the same type.

(b) T1 is a subrange of T2, or T2 is a subrange of T1, or both T1 and T2 are subranges of the same host type.

(c) T1 and T2 are set-types of compatible base-types, and either both T1 and T2 are designated packed or neither T1 nor T2 is designated packed.

(d) T1 and T2 are string-types with the same number of components.

6.4.6 *Assignment-Compatibility.* A value of type T2 shall be designated *assignment-compatible* with a type T1 if any of the following five statements is true.[62]

(a) T1 and T2 are the same type and that type is permissible as the component-type of a file-type (see 6.4.3.5).

(b) T1 is the real-type and T2 is the integer-type.

59. The type

```
file of CHAR
```

is thus not a synonym for the type

```
TEXT
```
.

One reason is that files of characters need not be organized into lines.

60. In the machine paradigm, identifying values are machine addresses and nil is a special non-address value. Pointer types are usually implemented this way.

61. The following pairs of types are compatible:

```
LEFTCOLUMN   = 1..10;
LINEPOSITION = 1..72;

LICENSEPREFIX = set of 'A'..'Z';
CONTROLCODES  = set of CHAR;

TEXTLINE = packed array [1..72] of CHAR;
ERRORLINE = packed array [1..72] of CHAR;
```

The rule (b) that a subrange type is compatible with its host type really makes a subrange type-wise equivalent to its host type. One exception to this generaization occurs for variable parameters (see Section 6.6.3.3) where formal and actual parameters must have the same type.

62. Notice that files values cannot be assigned. Notice also that integer numbers can be assigned to real variables but not vice versa.

(c) T1 and T2 are compatible ordinal-types and the value of type T2 is in the closed interval specified by the type T1.

(d) T1 and T2 are compatible set-types and all the members of the value of type T2 are in the closed interval specified by the base-type of T1.

(e) T1 and T2 are compatible string-types.

At any place where the rule of assignment-compatibility is used: **63**

(1) it shall be an error if T1 and T2 are compatible ordinal-types and the value of type T2 is not in the closed interval specified by type T1;

(2) it shall be an error if T1 and T2 are compatible set-types and any member of the value of type T2 is not in the closed interval specified by the base-type of the type T1.

6.4.7 *Example of a Type-Definition-Part*

```
type
   NATURAL    = 0..MAXINT;
   INDEXTYPE = 1..LIMIT;
   YEAR       = 1900..1999;
   COUNT      = INTEGER;
   RANGE      = INTEGER;

   COLOUR      = (RED, YELLOW, GREEN, BLUE); 64
   SEX         = (MALE, FEMALE);
   SHAPE       = (TRIANGLE, RECTANGLE, CIRCLE);
   PUNCHEDCARD = array [1..80] of CHAR;
   VECTOR      = array [INDEXTYPE] of REAL;

   CHARSEQUENCE = file of CHAR;
   POLAR        = record
                     R:     REAL;
                     THETA: ANGLE
                  end;

   PERSON       = ↑PERSONDETAILS;
   PERSONDETAILS =
     record
        NAME:      CHARSEQUENCE;
        FIRSTNAME: CHARSEQUENCE;
        AGE:       INTEGER;
        MARRIED:   BOOLEAN;
        FATHER:    PERSON;
        CHILD:     PERSON;
        SIBLING:   PERSON;
        case S: SEX of
           MALE:   (ENLISTED, BEARDED: BOOLEAN);
           FEMALE: (MOTHER, PROGRAMMER: BOOLEAN)
     end;
   FILEOFINTEGER = file of INTEGER;
```

63. For instance, with

```
type
   DAYNAME = (MONDAY, TUESDAY, WEDNESDAY,
              THURSDAY, FRIDAY,
              SATURDAY, SUNDAY);
   WEEKDAY = MONDAY .. FRIDAY;
var
   TODAY: WEEKDAY;
```

the statement

```
TODAY := MONDAY
```

is allowed but

```
TODAY := SUNDAY
```

is in error.

64. It is easy to forget the quite dramatic impact of Pascal's type facility when the language was introduced. Enumerated types, as symbolized by naming colors or days of the week and the general type facility exemplified here, were a winner.

NOTE. In the above example COUNT, RANGE and INTEGER denote the same type. The types denoted by YEAR and NATURAL are compatible with, but not the same as, the type denoted by RANGE, COUNT and INTEGER.[65]

65. These consequences follow from the rules given in 6.4.1 and 6.4.5.

6.5 DECLARATIONS AND DENOTATIONS OF VARIABLES

6.5.1 *Variable-Declarations.* A variable shall be an entity to which a value may be attributed (see 6.8.2.2). Each identifier in the identifier-list of a variable-declaration shall denote a distinct variable possessing the type denoted by the type-denoter of the variable-declaration.

> variable-declaration = identifier-list : type-denoter

The occurrence of an identifier in the identifier-list of a variable-declaration of the variable-declaration-part of a block shall constitute its defining-point as a variable-identifier for the region that is the block. The structure of a variable possessing a structured-type shall be the structure of the structured-type. A use of a variable-access shall be an access, at the time of the use, to the variable thereby denoted. A variable-access, according to whether it is an entire-variable, a component-variable, an identified-variable, or a buffer-variable, shall denote a declared variable, a component of a variable, a variable which is identified by a pointer value (see 6.4.4), or a buffer-variable, respectively.

> variable-access = entire-variable | component-variable
> | identified-variable | buffer-variable

Example of a variable-declaration-part:

```
var
    X, Y, Z, MAX: REAL;
    I, J:         INTEGER;
    P, Q, R:      BOOLEAN;
    K:            0..9;

    OPERATOR:     (PLUS, MINUS, TIMES);
    C:            COLOUR;
    F:            file of CHAR;
    HUE1, HUE2:   set of COLOUR;
    P1, P2:       PERSON;

    A:            array [0..63] of REAL;
    M, M1, M2:    array [1..10, 1..10] of REAL;
    POOLTAPE:     array [1..4] of FILEOFINTEGER;
    COORD:        POLAR:

    DATE:         record
                      MONTH: 1..12;
                      YEAR:  INTEGER
                  end;
```

NOTE. Variables occurring in examples in the remainder of this standard should be assumed to have been declared as specified in 6.5.1.

6.5.2 *Entire-Variables*

```
entire-variable     = variable-identifier
variable-identifier = identifier
```

6.5.3 *Component-Variables*

6.5.3.1 *General.* A component of a variable shall be a variable. A component-variable shall denote a component of a variable. A reference, or access to a component of a variable shall constitute a reference, or access, respectively, to the variable. The value, if any, of the component of a variable shall be the same component of the value, if any, of the variable.

```
component-variable = indexed-variable | field-designator
```

6.5.3.2 *Indexed-Variables.* A component of a variable possessing an array-type shall be denoted by an indexed-variable.

```
indexed-variable  = array-variable "[" index-expression [ ,
                      index-expression ]... "]"
array-variable    = variable-access
index-expression  = expression
```

An array-variable shall be a variable-access that denotes a variable possessing an array-type. For an indexed-variable closest-containing a single index-expression, the value of the index-expression shall be assignment-compatible with the index-type of the array-type. The component denoted by the indexed-variable shall be the component that corresponds to the value of the index-expression by the mapping of the type possessed by the array-variable (see 6.4.3.2).

Examples:
```
A[12]
A[I + J]
M[K]
```

If the array-variable is itself an indexed-variable an abbreviation may be used. In the abbreviated form, a single comma shall replace the sequence] [that occurs in the full form. The abbreviated form and the full form shall be equivalent.

The order of evaluation of the index-expressions of an indexed-variable shall be implementation-dependent. **66**

66. Consider the indexed variable

```
A[I, F(I)]
```

The actual subscript values will depend on the implementation if the call to F modifies I.

Examples:
```
M[K][1]
M[K,1]
```

NOTE. These two examples denote the same component variable.

6.5.3.3 *Field-Designators*.
A field-designator either shall denote that component of the record-variable of the field-designator associated with the field-identifier of the field-specifier of the field-designator, by the record-type possessed by the record-variable; or shall denote the variable denoted by the field-designator-identifier (see 6.8.3.10) of the field-designator. A record-variable shall be a variable-access that denotes a variable possessing a record-type.

The occurrence of a record-variable in a field-designator shall constitute the defining-point of the field-identifiers associated with components of the record-type possessed by the record-variable, for the region that is the field-specifier of the field-designator. [67]

```
field-designator     =  record-variable . field-specifier
                     |  field-designator-identifier

record-variable      =  variable-access
field-specifier      =  field-identifier
field-identifier     =  identifier
```

Examples:
```
P2↑.MOTHER
COORD.THETA
```

An access to a component of a variant of a variant-part, where the selector of the variant-part is not a field, shall attribute to the selector that value specified by its type associated with the variant.

It shall be an error unless a variant is active for the entirety of each reference and access to each component of the variant.

When a variant becomes not active, all of its components shall become totally-undefined. [68]

NOTE. If the selector of a variant-part is undefined, then no variant of the variant-part is active.

6.5.4 *Identified-Variables*.
An identifier-variable shall denote the variable (if any) identified by the value of the pointer-variable of the identifier-variable (see 6.4.4 and 6.6.5.3).

```
identified-variable  =  pointer-variable ↑
pointer-variable     =  variable-access
```

67. It is this rule which distinguishes a simple variable from a field identifier. The appearance of the record variable in a field designator "opens the scope" of the record so that its field identifiers are visible. Thus with the declarations

```
var
    A: REAL;
    R: record
            A: INTEGER;
            B: INTEGER
        end;
```

an assignment like

```
A := R.A
```

would assign the value of the A component of the record R to the simple variable A.

68. The value of the tag field determines which variant is active (see 6.4.3.3). In the absence of an explicit tag field, a reference to a component of a particular variant implicitly makes the referenced variant the active one. Once a given variant is active, the others are inactive.

A new variant can be made active (and the old one inactive) by either of the following: (a) assignment of a new record value with a different active variant, (b) assignment of a new value to an explicit tag field.

Consider the declarations

```
type
    VARIANTRECORD =
        record
            COUNT: INTEGER;
            case S: SEX of
                MALE:   (ENLISTED, BEARDED: BOOLEAN);
                FEMALE: (MOTHER, PROGRAMMER: BOOLEAN)
        end;
var
    A, B: VARIANTRECORD;
```

and the following statements:

```
A.S := FEMALE;
    { -- establishes an active variant for A }
A.ENLISTED := TRUE;
    { -- erroneous reference }
A.MOTHER := TRUE;
    { -- fine }
A.S := MALE;
    { -- A has a new active variant }
```

```
B.COUNT := 1;
  { -- B still has no active variant }
A := B;
  { -- A now has no active variant }
A.ENLISTED := TRUE;
  { -- erroneous reference }
B.S := MALE;
  { -- B now has an active variant }
A := B;
  { -- and so does A }
A.ENLISTED := TRUE;
  { -- valid reference }
```

We see here examples of active and inactive variants.

69. Even if a pointer variable is introduced in a nested procedure, any value associated with the pointer is potentially accessible during execution of the entire program. Consider

```
program POINTERS (INPUT, OUTPUT);
  type PTR = ↑INTEGER;
  var
    Q: PTR;
  procedure SETVALUE;
    var
      P: PTR;
    begin
      NEW(P);
      P↑ := 4;
      Q := P
    end;
begin
  NEW(Q);
  Q↑ := 2;
  SETVALUE;
  WRITE (Q↑)   { -- prints 4, not 2 }
end.
```

Here the value 4 associated with P in procedure SETVALUE remains accessible through the assignment of P to Q.

70. Notice that

```
P := nil;
Q := P↑  { -- in error }
```

and

```
NEW(P)
P↑ := 4;
Q := P;
DISPOSE (P);
WRITE (Q↑) { -- in error }
```

A variable created by the required procedure NEW (see 6.6.5.3) shall be accessible until the termination of the activation of the program-block [69] or until the variable is made inaccessible (see the required procedure DISPOSE, 6.6.5.3).

NOTE. The accessibility of the variable also depends on the existence of a pointer-variable that has attributed to it the corresponding identifying value.

A pointer-variable shall be a variable-access that denotes a variable possessing a pointer-type. It shall be an error if the pointer-variable of an identified-variable either denotes a nil-value or is undefined. It shall be an error to remove from its pointer-type the identifying-value of an identified variable (see 6.6.5.3) when a reference to the identified variable exists. [70]

Examples:

```
P1↑
P1↑.FATHER↑
P1↑.SIBLING↑.FATHER↑
```

6.5.5 *Buffer-Variables.* A file-variable shall be a variable-access that denotes a variable possessing a file-type. A buffer-variable shall denote a variable associated with the variable denoted by the file-variable of the buffer-variable. A buffer-variable associated with a textfile shall possess the char-type; otherwise, a buffer-variable shall possess the component-type of the file-type possessed by the file-variable of the buffer-variable.

```
buffer-variable  =  file-variable ↑
file-variable    =  variable-access
```

Examples:

```
INPUT↑
POOLTAPE[2]↑
```

It shall be an error to alter the value of a file-variable f when a reference to the buffer-variable f↑ exists. A reference or access to a buffer-variable shall constitute a reference or access, respectively, to the associated file-variable. [71]

6.6 PROCEDURE AND FUNCTION DECLARATIONS

6.6.1 *Procedure-Declarations*

procedure-declaration	=	procedure-heading ; directive
	|	procedure-identification ; procedure-block
	|	procedure-heading ; procedure-block
procedure-heading	=	procedure identifier [formal-parameter-list]
procedure-identification	=	procedure procedure-identifier
procedure-identifier	=	identifier
procedure-block	=	block

The occurrence of a formal-parameter-list in a procedure-heading of a procedure-declaration shall define the formal parameters of the procedure-block, if any, associated with the identifier of the procedure-heading to be those of the formal-parameter-list.

The occurrence of an identifier in the procedure-heading of a procedure-declaration shall constitute its defining-point as a procedure-identifier for the region that is the block closest-containing the procedure-declaration.

Each identifier having a defining-point as a procedure-identifier in a procedure-heading of a procedure-declaration closest-containing the directive FORWARD [72] shall have exactly one of its applied occurrences in a procedure-identification of a procedure-declaration, and that shall be closest-contained by the procedure-and-function-declaration-part closest-containing the procedure-heading.

The occurrence of a procedure-block in a procedure-declaration shall associate the procedure-block with the identifier in the procedure-heading, or with the procedure-identifier in the procedure-identification, of the procedure-declaration.

Example of a procedure-and-function-declaration-part:

```
procedure READINTEGER (var F: TEXT;
                       var X: INTEGER);
   var
      I: NATURAL;
   begin
      while F↑ = ' ' do
         GET(F);
      { -- The file buffer contains the first non-space char }

      I := 0;
      while F↑ in ['0'..'9'] do begin
         I := (10 * I) + (ORD(F↑) - ORD('0'));
         GET(F)
      end;
      { -- The file buffer contains a non-digit }

      X := I
      { -- Of course if there are no digits, X is zero }
   end;


procedure BISECT (function F(X: REAL): REAL;
                  A, B: REAL;
                  var RESULT: REAL);
   { -- This procedure attempts to find a zero of F(X) in (A,B) by the
     -- method of bisection. It is assumed that the procedure is called
     -- with suitable values of A and B such that
     --    (F(A) < 0) and (F(B) > 0)
     -- The estimate is returned in the last parameter. }
```

are in error. Notice also that DISPOSE cannot be appied to a pointer variable if a reference to the identified variable exists. Thus in

```
NEW(P);
SETUP(P);
DOTHIS (P↑)
```

the procedure DOTHIS cannot dispose of P.

71. The error mentioned can arise in a procedure call such as

```
UPDATE (F, F↑)
```

where the file F might be reset while the window F↑ refers to a medial component.

72. A procedure declared as FORWARD must have its full definition given in the same declarative part.

```
        const
          EPS = 1E-10;
        var
          MIDPOINT: REAL;

  begin
    { -- The invariant P is true by calling assumption }
    MIDPOINT := A;

    while ABS(A - B) > EPS * ABS(A) do begin
      MIDPOINT := (A + B) / 2;
      if F(MIDPOINT) < 0 then
        A := MIDPOINT
      else
        B := MIDPOINT
        { -- Which re-establishes the invariant:
          --    P = (F(A) < 0) and (F(B) > 0)
          -- and reduces the interval (A,B) provided that the value of
          -- MIDPOINT is distinct from both A and B. }
    end;

    { -- P together with the loop exit condition assures that a zero is
      -- contained in a small sub-interval. Return the midpoint as the
      -- zero. }
    RESULT := MIDPOINT
  end;



procedure PREPAREFORAPPENDING (var F: FILEOFINTEGER);
    { -- This procedure takes a file in an arbitrary state and sets it up
      -- in a condition for appending data to its end. Simpler conditioning
      -- is only possible if assumptions are made about the initial state
      -- of the file. }

    var
      LOCALCOPY: FILEOFINTEGER;


    procedure COPYFILES (var FROM, INTO: FILEOFINTEGER);
    begin
      RESET (FROM);
      REWRITE (INTO);
      while not EOF(FROM) do begin
        INTO↑ := FROM↑;
        PUT (INTO);
        GET (FROM)
      end
    end { -- of COPYFILES };

begin { -- of body of PREPAREFORAPPENDING }
  COPYFILES (F, LOCALCOPY);
  COPYFILES (LOCALCOPY, F)
end   { -- of PREPAREFORAPPENDING };
```

6.6.2 *Function-Declarations*

```
function-declaration   =   function-heading ; directive
                       |   function-identification ; function-block
                       |   function-heading ; function-block

function-heading       =   function identifier [ formal-parameter-list ] :
                           result-type

function-identification   =   function function-identifier

function-identifier    =   identifier
result-type            =   simple-type-identifier
                       |   pointer-type-identifier
function-block         =   block
```

The occurrence of a formal-parameter-list in a function-heading of a function-declaration shall define the formal parameters of the function-block, if any, associated with the identifier of the function-heading to be those of the formal-parameter-list. The function-block shall contain at least one assignment-statement such that the function-identifier of the assignment-statement is associated with the block (see 6.8.2.2). [73]

The occurrence of an identifier in the function-heading of a function-declaration shall constitute its defining-point as a function-identifier associated with the result type denoted by the result-type for the region that is the block closest-containing the function-declaration.

Each identifier having a defining-point as a function-identifier in the function-heading of a function-declaration closest-containing the directive FORWARD shall have exactly one of its applied occurrences in a function-identification of a function-declaration, and that shall be closest-contained by the procedure-and-function-declaration-part closest-containing the function-heading. [74]

The occurrence of a function-block in a function-declaration shall associate the function-block with the identifier in the function-heading, or with the function-identifier in the function-identification, of the function-declaration; the block of the function-block shall be associated with the result type that is associated with the identifier or function-identifier, respectively.

Example of a procedure-and-function-declaration-part:

```
function SQRT (X: REAL): REAL;
   { -- This function computes the square root of X (X > 0)
     -- using Newton's method. }
   var
      OLD, ESTIMATE: REAL;
```

73. A function may have an empty parameter list. For recursively defined functions, we may even have something like

```
function F: { -- returns } INTEGER;
   { -- local declarations }
begin
   ...
   F := F + 1;
   ...
end;
```

In cases like this, the occurrence of F on the right side of the assignment denotes recursive call to F, and that on the left side of a return value to F.

74. A forward declaration specifies all of the type properties needed to type-check calls to a function or procedure. For example, we may have

```
function MEDIAN (T: TABLE): REAL;
   FORWARD;
```

where the body is given later in the same declarative part. This facility is used mainly to make mutual recursion possible, as in the examples to follow. It may also be used to group function and procedure headings at the beginning of a long declarative part.

```
begin
   ESTIMATE := X;
   REPEAT
      OLD := ESTIMATE;
      ESTIMATE := (OLD + X / OLD) * 0.5;
   until ABS(ESTIMATE - OLD) < EPS * ESTIMATE;
   { -- EPS being a global constant }
   SQRT := ESTIMATE
end { -- of SQRT };


function MAX (A: VECTOR): REAL;
   { -- This function finds the largest component of the value of A. }
   var
      LARGESTSOFAR: REAL;
      FENCE: INDEXTYPE;
begin
   LARGESTSOFAR := A[1];
   { -- Establishes LARGESTSOFAR = MAX(A[1]) }

   for FENCE := 2 to LIMIT do begin
      if LARGESTSOFAR < A[FENCE] then
         LARGESTSOFAR := A[FENCE]
      { -- Re-establishing LARGESTSOFAR = MAX(A[1], ... ,A[FENCE]) }
   end;
   { -- So now LARGESTSOFAR = MAX(A[1], ... ,A[LIMIT]) }

   MAX := LARGESTSOFAR
end { -- of MAX };


function GCD (M, N: NATURAL): NATURAL;
begin
   if N = 0 then
      GCD := M
   else
      GCD := GCD(N, M mod N);
end;
```

{ -- The following two functions analyse a parenthesized expression and
      convert it to an internal form. They are declared FORWARD since they
      are mutually recursive, [75] i.e. they call each other. }

75. Here, only READOPERAND strictly needs to be declared as FORWARD.

```
function READEXPRESSION: FORMULA;
   FORWARD;
function READOPERAND: FORMULA;
   FORWARD;

function READEXPRESSION; { -- See FORWARD declaration of heading. }
   var
      THIS: FORMULA;
      OP:   OPERATION;
```

```
begin
   THIS := READOPERAND;
   while ISOPERATOR(NEXTSYM) do begin
      OP := READOPERATOR;
      THIS := MAKEFORMULA(THIS, OP, READOPERAND);
   end;
   READEXPRESSION := THIS
end;

function READOPERAND; { -- See FORWARD declaration of heading. }
begin
   if ISOPENPARENTHESIS(NEXTSYM) then
      begin
         SKIPSYMBOL;
         READOPERAND := READEXPRESSION;
         { -- NEXTSYM should be a close-parenthesis }
         SKIPSYMBOL
      end
   else
      READOPERAND := READELEMENT
end;
```

6.6.3 *Parameters*

6.6.3.1 *General.* The identifier-list in a value-parameter-specification shall be a list of value parameters. The identifier-list in a variable-parameter-specification shall be a list of variable parameters.

formal-parameter-list	=	(formal-parameter-section [; formal-parameter-section]...)
formal-parameter-section	=	value-parameter-specification | variable-parameter-specification | procedural-parameter-specification | functional-parameter-specification

value-parameter-specification	=	identifier-list : type-identifier
variable-parameter-specification	=	var identifier-list : type-identifier
procedural-parameter-specification	=	procedure-heading
functional-parameter-specification	=	function-heading

An identifier defined to be a parameter-identifier for the region that is the formal-parameter-list of a procedure-heading shall be designated a formal parameter of the block of the procedure-block, if any, associated with the identifier of the procedure-heading. An identifier defined to be a parameter-identifier for the region that is the formal-parameter-list of a function-heading shall be designated a formal parameter of the block of the function-block, if any, associated with the identifier of the function-heading.

76. The scope of a formal parameter covers the entire formal parameter list (i.e. no two formal parameters may have the same identifier) and the body of the procedure (i.e. except for nested units, the parameter cannot be redeclared in the same body).

The scope of the procedure identifier itself is the containing block (see 6.6.1). Accordingly, a formal parameter can have the same identifier as the procedure itself, as in

```
procedure X (X: INTEGER);
begin
   WRITE (X) { -- the formal parameter }
end
```

In these cases, recursive calls (say to procedure X) are not allowed. For functions, the above scenario breaks down since it would be impossible to assign a return value to the function identifier within the function body.

Normally a function or procedure has an associated block. The phrase "if any" recurs frequently and is used to cover cases where the parameter is itself part of a function or procedure parameter, as in

```
procedure P (function F(X,Y: REAL): REAL);
begin
   . . .
end;
```

Here X and Y have no associated block. Their scope is only the formal parameter list. Hence X and Y must be different identifiers. Otherwise, the parameter names have no effect, as they do not appear in the body of P.

77. Note that in cases like

```
procedure P (var X: INTEGER);
begin
   I := 1;
   X := X + 1;
end;
. . .
I := 2
P (A[I]) { -- A[2], not A[1], is updated }
```

the actual parameter is established before the procedure is called.

The occurrence of an identifier in the identifier-list of a value-parameter-specification or a variable-parameter-specification shall constitute its defining-point as a parameter-identifier for the region that is the formal-parameter-list closest-containing it and its defining-point as the associated variable-identifier for the region that is the block, if any, of which it is a formal parameter. **76**

The occurrence of the identifier of a procedure-heading in a procedural-parameter-specification shall constitute its defining-point as a parameter-identifier for the region that is the formal parameter-list closest-containing it and its defining-point as the associated procedure-identifier for the region that is the block, if any, of which it is a formal parameter.

The occurrence of the identifier of a function-heading in a functional-parameter-specification shall constitute its defining-point as a parameter-identifier for the region that is the formal-parameter-list closest-containing it and its defining-point as the associated function-identifier for the region that is the block, if any, of which it is a formal parameter.

NOTE. If the formal-parameter-list is contained in a procedural-parameter-specification or a functional-parameter-specification, there is no corresponding procedure-block or function-block.

6.6.3.2 *Value Parameters.* The formal parameter and its associated variable-identifier shall denote the same variable. The formal parameter shall possess the type denoted by the type-identifier of the value-parameter-specification. The type possessed by a formal parameter shall be one that is permitted as the component-type of a file-type. The actual-parameter (see 6.7.3 and 6.8.2.3) shall be an expression whose value is assignment-compatible with the type possessed by the formal parameter. The current value of the expression shall be attributed upon activation of the block to the variable that is denoted by the formal parameter.

6.6.3.3 *Variable Parameters.* The actual-parameter shall be a variable-access. The type possessed by the actual-parameters shall be the same as that denoted by the type-identifier of the variable-parameter-specification, and the formal parameters shall also possess that type. The actual-parameter shall be accessed before the activation of the block, and this access shall establish a reference to the variable thereby accessed during the entire activation of the block; **77** the corresponding formal parameter and its associated variable-identifier shall denote the referenced variable during the activation.

An actual variable parameter shall not denote a field that is the selector of a variant-part. **78** An actual variable parameter shall not denote a component of a variable where that variable possesses a type that is designated packed. **79**

6.6.3.4 *Procedural Parameters.* The actual-parameter (see 6.7.3 and 6.8.2.3) shall be a procedure-identifier that has a defining-point contained by the program-block. **80** The procedure denoted by the actual-parameter and the procedure denoted by the formal parameter shall have congruous formal-parameter-lists (see 6.6.3.6) if either has a formal-parameter-list. The formal parameter and its associated procedure-identifier shall denote the actual parameter during the entire activation of the block.

6.6.3.5 *Functional Parameters.* The actual-parameter (see 6.7.3 and 6.8.2.3) shall be a function-identifier that has a defining-point contained by the program-block. The function denoted by the actual-parameter and the function denoted by the formal parameter shall have the same result-type and shall have congruous formal-parameter-lists (see 6.6.3.6) if either has a formal-parameter-list. The formal parameter and its associated function-identifier shall denote the actual parameter during the entire activation of the block.

NOTE. Since required procedures and functions are used as if their defining-points have a region enclosing the program (see 6.2.2.10), these procedures and functions may not be used as actual parameters in a program.

6.6.3.6 *Parameter List Congruity.* Two formal-parameter-lists shall be congruous if they contain the same number of formal-parameter-sections and if the formal-parameter-sections in corresponding positions match. **81** Two formal-parameter-sections shall match if any of the following statements is true.

(a) They are both value-parameter-specifications containing the same number of parameters and the type-identifier in each value-parameter-specification denotes the same type.

(b) They are both variable-parameter-specifications containing the same number of parameters and the type-identifier in each variable-parameter-specification denotes the same type.

(c) They are both procedural-parameter-specifications and the formal-parameter-lists of the procedure-headings thereof are congruous.

(d) They are both functional-parameter-specifications, the formal-parameter-lists of the function-headings are congruous, and the type-identifiers of the result-types of the function-headings thereof denote the same type.

6.6.4 Required Procedures and Functions

6.6.4.1 *General.* The required procedure-identifiers and function-identifiers and the corresponding required procedures and functions shall be as specified in 6.6.5 and 6.6.6, respectively.

78. Passing the tag field as a variable would leave open many difficult implementation issues and is thus forbidden.

79. Violating this would leave open the possibility of a formal parameter that could in one call refer to a component of a packed structure and in another call to an unpacked structure. This possibility can be costly to implement and is thus forbidden.

80. This prevents the passing of procedure arguments defined externally to the program, as well as passing of the required procedures like READ or PAGE as arguments (see Section 6.2.2.10).

81. The key idea here is that type of corresponding parameters is the same. Thus the formal parameter

```
procedure P (C: COLUMN)
```

is an acceptable match for

```
procedure Q (D: COLUMN)
```

but not for

```
procedure Q (C: INTEGER)
```

or

```
procedure Q (var D: COLUMN)
```

Note that

```
procedure R (X,Y: REAL)
```

does not match

```
procedure S (X:REAL; Y:REAL)
```

6.6.5. *Required Procedures*

82. The use of assertions to explain what happens when a procedure is called deserves a comment. A "pre-assertion" describes the state of the file and some properties that must hold for the procedure to be called without error. The corresponding "post-assertion" states the net result of the procedure call.

83. REWRITE can be applied to any file (except INPUT) at any time. It sets the file to have empty left and right parts, and prepares the file for writing new values. The buffer variable F↑ has, of course, no value.

84. PUT can only be applied to files in writing mode and the buffer variable F↑ must have been assigned a value. A call to PUT appends the value of F↑ to the end of the file. Since a file in writing mode always has an empty right part, the value is appended to the left part.

85. Notice that RESET can only be applied to files with defined values. This can mean an existing file or a newly created file defined by a call to REWRITE. A call to REWRITE establishes an empty file (which is not the same as undefined).

Basically RESET resets a file so that its values can be read and puts the first value in the buffer variable F↑. If the file happens to be empty then F↑ is undefined. The appearance of X in the definition serves to attach an end-of-line if the file happens to be a textfile with a partial last line.

6.6.5.1 *General.* The required procedures shall be file handling procedures, dynamic allocation procedures and transfer procedures.

6.6.5.2 *File Handling Procedures.* Except for the application of REWRITE or RESET to the program parameters denoted by INPUT or OUTPUT, the effects of applying each of the file handling procedures REWRITE, PUT, RESET and GET to a file-variable f shall be defined by pre-assertions and post-assertions [82] after f, its components f.L, f.R, and f.M, and about the associated buffer-variable f↑. The use of the variable f0 within an assertion shall be considered to represent the state or value, as appropriate, of f prior to the operation, while f (within an assertion) shall denote the variable after the operation, and similarly for f0↑ and f↑.

It shall be an error if the stated pre-assertion does not hold immediately prior to any use of the defined operation. It shall be an error if any variable explicitly denoted in an assertion of equality is undefined. The post-assertion shall hold prior to the next subsequent access to the file, its components, or its associated buffer-variable. The post-assertions imply corresponding activities on the external entities, if any, to which the file-variables are bound. These activities, and the point at which they are actually performed, shall be implementation-defined.

REWRITE(f) [83]
pre-assertion:	TRUE
post-assertion:	(f.L = f.R = S()) and (f.M = Generation) and (f01↑ is totally-undefined)

PUT(f) [84]
pre-assertion	(f0.M = Generation) and (f0.L is not undefned) and (f0.R = S()) and (f0↑ is not undefined)
post-assertion:	(f.M = Generation) and (f.L = (f0.L · S(f0↑))) and (f.R = S()) and (f↑ is totally-undefined)

RESET(f) [85]
pre-assertion:	The components f0.L and f0.R are not undefined.
post-assertion:	(f.L = S()) and (f.R = (f0.L · f0.R · X)) and

(f.M = Inspection) and
(if f.R = S() then (f↑ is totally-undefined)
  else (f↑ = f.R.first))

where, if f possesses the type denoted by the required structured-type-identifier TEXT and if f0.L • f0.R is not empty and if (f0.L • f0.R).last is not designated an end-of-line, then X shall be a sequence having an end-of-line component as its only component; otherwise X = S()

GET(f) **86**

pre-assertion: (f0.M = Inspection) and
              (neither f0.L nor f0.R are undefined) and
              (f0.R <> S())

post-assertion: (f.M = Inspection) and
              (f.L = (f0.L • S(f0.R.first))) and
              (f.R = f0.R.rest) and
              (if f.R = S() then (f↑ is totally-undefined)
              else (f↑ = f.R.first))

86. GET can only be applied to a file with more data in it. GET sets the buffer variable F↑ to hold the next file component and appends this component to the left part so that subsequent calls will read a new component into F↑.

When the file-variable f possesses a type other than that denoted by text, the required procedures READ and WRITE shall be defined as follows.

READ

Let f denote a file-variable and v1 ... vn denote variable-accesses; then the procedure-statement READ(f, v1, ... ,vn) shall access the file variable and establish a reference to the file variable for the remaining execution of the statement. The execution of the statement shall be equivalent to

```
begin
   READ(ff, v1);
   READ(ff, v2, ..., vn)
end
```

where ff denotes the referenced file variable. The READ statement containing v1 shall be executed before accessing the variables v2, ... ,vn.

Let f be a file-variable and v be a variable-access; then the procedure statement READ(f, v) shall access the file variable and establish a reference to that file variable for the remaining execution of the statement. The execution of the statement shall be equivalent to

```
begin
   v := ff↑;
   GET(ff)
end
```

where ff denotes the referenced file variable. **87**

NOTE. The variable-access is not a variable parameter. Consequently it may be a component of a packed structure and the value of the buffer-variable need only be assignment-compatible with it.

87. The use of the intermediate file variable ff in the definition is deliberate. It means that side-effects that may arise out of expressions in the call shall not alter reference to the single file variable. This might happen if the file variable is an element of an array.

WRITE

Let f denote a file-variable and e1 ... en denote expressions; then the procedure-statement WRITE(f, e1, ... ,en) shall access the file variable and establish a reference to that file variable for the remaining execution of the statement. The execution of the statement shall be equivalent to

```
begin
    WRITE(ff, e1);
    WRITE(ff, e2, ..., en)
end
```

where ff denotes the referenced file variable. The WRITE statement containing e1 shall be executed before evaluating the expressions e2, ... ,en.

Let f be a file-variable and e be an expression; then the procedure-statement WRITE(f, e) shall access the file variable and establish a reference to that file variable for the remaining execution of the statement. The execution of the WRITE statement shall be equivalent to

```
begin
    ff↑ := e;
    PUT(ff)
end
```

where ff denotes the referenced file variable.

NOTES
1. The required procedures READ, WRITE, READLN, WRITELN, and PAGE, as applied to textfiles, are described in 6.9.
2. Since the definitions of READ and WRITE include the use of GET and PUT, the implementation-defined aspects of their post-assertions also apply.

6.6.5.3 *Dynamic Allocation Procedures*

NEW(p)

shall create a new variable that is totally-undefined, shall create a new identifying-value of the pointer-type associated with p, that identifies the new variable, and shall attribute this identifying value to the variable denoted by the variable-access p. The created variable shall possess the type that is the domain-type of the pointer-type possessed by p. [88]

88. NEW creates a dynamic variable with an undefined value. Any value subsequently associated with the variable must have the domain type of the pointer type.

NEW(p,c1, ... ,cn)

shall create a new variable that is totally-undefined, shall create a new identifying-value of the pointer-type associated with p, that identifies the new variable, and shall attribute this identifying-value to the variable denoted by the variable-access p. The created variable shall possess the record-type that is the domain-type of the pointer-type possessed by p and shall have nested variants that correspond to the case-constants c1, ... ,cn. The case-constants shall be listed in order of increasing nesting of the variant-parts. Any variant not specified shall be listed in order of increasing nesting of the variant-parts. Any variant not specified shall be at a deeper level of nesting than that specified by cn. It shall be an error if a variant of a variant-part within the new variable becomes active and a different variant of the variant-part is one of the specified variants. [89]

DISPOSE(q) shall remove the identifying-value denoted by the expression q from the pointer-type of q. It shall be an error if the identifying-value had been created using the form NEW(p, c1, ... ,cn).

DISPOSE(q,k1, ... ,km) shall remove the identifying-value denoted by the expression q from the pointer-type of q. The case-constants k1, ... ,km shall be listed in order of increasing nesting of the variant-parts. It shall be an error if the variable had been created using the form NEW(p, c1, ... ,cn) and m is not equal to n. It shall be an error if the variants in the variable identified by the pointer-value of q are different from those specified by the case-constants k1, ... ,km. [90]

NOTE. The removal of an identifying-value from the pointer-type to which it belongs renders the identified variable inaccessible (see 6.5.4) and makes undefined [91] all variables and functions that have that value attributed (see 6.6.3.2 and 6.6.2.2).

It shall be an error if q has a nil-value or is undefined.

It shall be an error if a variable created using the second form of NEW is accessed by the identified-variable of the variable-access of a factor, of an assignment-statement, or of an actual-parameter.

6.6.5.4 *Transfer Procedures.* Let a be a variable possessing an array-type, and let s1 denote the index-type thereof, let z be a variable possessing an array-type designated packed, let s2 denote the index-type thereof, and let the array-types have the same component-type; let u and v be the smallest and largest values of the type s2, let i be an expression whose value is assignment-compatible with s1, and let j and k denote auxiliary variables which the program does not otherwise contain. The type possessed by j shall be s2; the type possessed by k shall be s1.

The statement PACK(a, i, z) shall access the array variables a and z and establish references to these variables for the remaining execution of the statement. The execution of the statement shall be equivalent to [92]

```
begin
   k := i;
   for j := u to v do
      begin
         zz[j] := aa[k];
         if j <> v then k := SUCC(k)
      end
end
```

89. Record variants created by this use of NEW are quite restricted. For one, the tag values c1 through cn must be given as constants. The record variable is then frozen to take on only the specified variants. Such a record variable may not be assigned a completely new value nor be passed as a parameter. And, of course, the tag fields cannot be changed.

90. The use of this form of DISPOSE is restricted. The case constants must match exactly (the same number and the same values) as that used in the corresponding call to NEW. You cannot say

```
NEW(RECORDVAR, TAGVALUE1)
```

and later say

```
DISPOSE(RECORDVAR)
```

91. DISPOSE allows the space allocated to a dynamic variable created by NEW to be reused. Any other references to the freed value have undefined values. For example, in

```
NEW(P);
P↑ := 2;
Q := P;
DISPOSE(P)
```

the value associated with Q becomes undefined. Notice that a Pascal implementation is not actually *required* to reclaim the disposed space.

92. Essentially

```
PACK(A, I, Z)
```

means pack array Z with the components of A starting with A[I]. Notice that A must have enough components to fill Z. The call

```
UNPACK(Z, A, I)
```

means unpack the array Z into the components of A starting with A[I].

where aa denotes the referenced unpacked array variable and zz denotes the referenced packed array variable.

The statement UNPACK(z, a, ı) shall access the array variables a and z and establish references to these variables for the remaining execution of the statement. The execution of the statement shall be equivalent to

```
begin
    k := i;
    for j := u to v do
        begin
            aa[k] := zz[j];
            if j <> v then k := SUCC(k)
        end
end
```

where aa denotes the referenced unpacked array variable and zz denotes the referenced packed array variable.

6.6.6 *Required Functions*

6.6.6.1 *General.* The required functions shall be arithmetic functions, transfer functions, ordinal functions and Boolean functions.

6.6.6.2 *Arithmetic Functions.* For the following arithmetic functions, the expression x shall be either of real-type or integer-type. For the functions ABS and SQR, the type of the result shall be the same as the type of the parameter x. For the remaining arithmetic functions, the result shall always be of real-type.

Function	*Result*
ABS(x)	shall compute the absolute value of x.
SQR(x)	shall compute the square of x. It shall be an error if such a value does not exist.
SIN(x)	shall compute the sine of x, where x is in radians.
COS(x)	shall compute the cosine of x, where x is in radians.
EXP(x)	shall compute the value of the base of natural logarithms raised to the power x.
LN(x)	shall compute the natural logarithm of x, if x is greater than zero. It shall be an error if x is not greater than zero.
SQRT(x)	shall compute the non-negative square root of x, if x is not negative. It shall be an error if x is negative.

ARCTAN(x)   shall compute the principal value, in radians, of the arctangent of x.

6.6.6.3 *Transfer Functions.*

TRUNC(x)   From the expression x that shall be of real-type, this function shall return a result of integer-type. The value of TRUNC(x) shall be such that if x is positive or zero then

$$0 \; <= \; x - \text{TRUNC}(x) \; < \; 1;$$

otherwise

$$-1 \; < \; x - \text{TRUNC}(x) \; <= \; 0$$

It shall be an error if such a value does not exist.

Examples:
TRUNC(3.5)   yields 3
TRUNC(-3.5)   yields -3

ROUND(x)   From the expression x that shall be of real-type, this function shall return a result of integer-type. If x is positive or zero, ROUND(x) shall be equivalent to TRUNC(x + 0.5), otherwise ROUND(x) shall be equivalent to TRUNC(x – 0.5). It shall be an error if such a value does not exist.

Examples:
ROUND(3.5)   yields 4
ROUND(-3.5)   yields -4

6.6.6.4 *Ordinal Functions.*

ORD(x)   From the expression x that shall be of an ordinal-type, this function shall return a result of integer-type that shall be the ordinal number (see 6.4.2.2 and 6.4.2.3) of the value of the expression x.

CHR(x)   From the expression x that shall be of integer-type, this function shall return a result of char-type that shall be the value whose ordinal number is equal to the value of the expression x if such a character value exists. It shall be an error if such a character value does not exist.

For any value, ch, of char-type, it shall be true that:

CHR(ORD(ch)) = ch

SUCC(x)   From the expression x that shall be of an ordinal-type, this function shall return a result that shall be of the same type as that of the expression (see 6.7.1). The function shall yield a value whose ordinal number is one greater than that of the expression x, if such a value exists. It shall be an error if such a value does not exist.

PRED(x)   From the expression x that shall be of an ordinal-type, this function shall return a result that shall be of the same type as that of the expression (see 6.7.1). The function shall yield a value whose ordinal number is one less than that of the expression x, if such a value exists. It shall be an error if such a value does not exist.

6.6.6.5 *Boolean Functions.*

ODD(x)   From the expression x that shall be of integer-type, this function shall be equivalent to the expression (ABS(x) mod 2 = 1).

EOF(f)   The parameter f shall be a file-variable; if the actual-parameter-list is omitted, the function shall be applied to the required textfile INPUT (see 6.10). When EOF(f) is activated, it shall be an error if f is undefined; otherwise the function shall yield the value TRUE is f.R is the empty sequence (see 6.4.3.5), otherwise FALSE.

EOLN(f)   The parameter f shall be a textfile; if the actual-parameter-list is omitted, the function shall be applied to the required textfile INPUT (see 6.10). When EOLN(f) is activated, it shall be an error if f is undefined or if EOF(f) is true; otherwise the function shall yield the value TRUE if f.R.first is an end-of-line component (see 6.4.3.5), otherwise FALSE.

6.7 EXPRESSIONS

6.7.1 *General.* An expression shall denote a value unless a variable denoted by a variable-access contained by the expression is undefined at the time of its use, in which case that use shall be an error. The use of a variable-access as a factor shall denote the value, if any, attributed to the variable accessed thereby. Operator precedences shall be according to four classes of operators as follows. The operator *not* shall have the highest precedence, followed by the multiplying-operators, then the adding-operators and signs, and finally, with the lowest precedence, the relational-operators. [93] Sequences of two or more operators of the same precedence shall be left associative.

93. Because of the mixing of Boolean operators with arithmetic operators in a single precedence level, care must be taken when they appear together. For instance you cannot write

if TODAY = MONDAY or TODAY = TUESDAY then

or

if X1 < X2 and Y1 < Y2 then

These must be written

if (TODAY = MONDAY) or (TODAY = TUESDAY) then
if (X1 < X2) and (Y1 < Y2) then

expression = simple-expression [relational-operator simple-expression]...

simple-expression = [sign] term [adding-operator term]...

term = factor [multiplying-operator factor]...

factor = variable-access | unsigned-constant
         | function-designator | set-constructor
         | (expression) | not factor

unsigned-constant = unsigned-number | character-string
                    | constant-identifier | nil

```
set-constructor      = "["[member-designator[,member-designator]...]"]"
member-designator = expression [ .. expression ]
```

Any factor whose type is S, where S is a subrange of T, shall be treated as of type T. Similarly, any factor whose type is set of S shall be treated as of the unpacked canonical set-of-T type, and any factor whose type is packed set of S shall be treated as of the packed canonical set-of-T type.

NOTE. Consequently, an expression that consists of a single factor of type S is itself of type T, and an expression that consists of a single factor of type S is itself of type set of T, and an expression that consists of a single factor of type packed set of S is itself of type packed set of T.

A set-constructor shall denote a value of a set-type. The set-constructor [] shall denote that value in every set-type that contains no members. A set-constructor containing one or more member-designators shall denote either a value of the unpacked canonical set-of-T type, or if the context so requires, the packed canonical set-of-T type, where T is the type of every expression of each member-designator of the set-constructor. The type T shall be an ordinal-type. The value denoted by the set-constructor shall contain zero or more members each of which shall be denoted by at least one member-designator of the set-constructor.

The member-designator x, where x is an expression, shall denote the member that shall have the value x. The member-designator x..y, where x and y are expressions, shall denote zero or more members that shall have the values of the base-type in the closed interval from the value of x to the value of y. The order of evaluation of the expressions of a member-designator shall be implementation-dependent. The order of evaluation of the member-designators of a set-constructor shall be implementation-dependent.

NOTE. The member-designator x..y denotes no members if the value of x is greater than the value of y.

Examples:

(a) Factors:
```
X
15
(X + Y + Z)
SIN(X + Y)
[RED, C, GREEN]
[1, 5, 10..19, 23]
not P
```

(b) Terms:
```
X * Y
I / (1 - I)
(X <= Y) and (Y < Z)
```

(c) Simple Expressions:
```
P or Q
X + Y
-X
HUE1 + HUE2
I * J + 1
```

(d) Expressions: X = 1.5
                  P <= Q
                  P = Q and R
                  (I < J) = (J < K)
                  C in HUE1

6.7.2 *Operators*

6.7.2.1 *General*

multiplying-operator = * | / | div | mod | and

adding-operator   = + | – | or

relational-operator   = = | <> | < | > | <= | >= | in

A factor, or a term, or a simple-expression shall be designated an operand. The order of evaluation of the operands of a dyadic operator shall be implementation-dependent.

NOTE. This means, for example, that the operands may be evaluated in textual order, or in reverse order, or in parallel or they may not both be evaluated. **94**

6.7.2.2 *Arithmetic Operators.* The types of operands and results for dyadic and monadic operations shall be as shown in Tables 2 and 3, respectively.

94. For instance, in

```
if (X < 1.0) or (Y / X > 1.0) then
```

both alternatives need not be evaluated, so if X is 0.0 the result is up to the implementation. It also means that in

```
if (F(X) < 1.0) or (G(X) < 1.0) then
```

the order of any side-effects is implementation-dependent.

95. Some examples:

```
6.0 + 1    7.0  { -- result is REAL }
6.0 * 2   12.0  { -- result is REAL }
6 / 2      3.0  { -- result is REAL }

7 div 2    3    { -- result is INTEGER }
-7 div -2  3    { -- result is INTEGER }

7 mod 2    1    { -- remainder after division }
-7 mod 2   1    { -- not -1 }
7 mod -2   _    { -- in error }
```

TABLE 2 **95**
Dyadic Arithmetic Operations

Operator	Operation	Type of Operands	Type of result
+	addition	integer-type or real-type	(1)
–	subtraction	integer-type or real-type	(1)
*	multiplication	integer-type or real-type	(1)
/	division	integer-type or real-type	real-type
div	division with truncation	integer-type	integer-type
mod	modulo	integer-type	integer-type

(1) Integer-type if both operands are of integer-type, otherwise real-type.

TABLE 3
Monadic Arithmetic Operations

Operator	Operation	Type of Operand	Type of Result
+	identity	integer-type real-type	integer-type real-type
−	sign-inversion	integer-type real-type	integer-type real-type

NOTE. The symbols +, −, and * are also used as set operators (see 6.7.2.4).

A term of the form x/y shall be an error if y is zero, otherwise the value of x/y shall be the result of dividing x by y.

A term of the form i div j shall be an error if j is zero, otherwise the value of i div j shall be such that

```
ABS(i) − ABS(j)  <  ABS((i div j) * j)  <=  ABS(i)
```

where the value shall be zero if ABS(i) < ABS(j), otherwise the sign of the value shall be positive if i and j have the same sign and negative if i and j have different signs.

A term of the form i mod j shall be an error if j is zero or negative, otherwise the value of i mod j shall be that value of (i−(k*j)) for integral k such that 0 <= i mod j < j.

NOTE. Only for i >= 0 and j > 0 does the relation (i div j) * j + i mod j = i hold.

The required constant-identifier MAXINT shall denote an implementation-defined value of integer-type. This value shall satisfy the following conditions.

(a) All integral values in the closed interval from −MAXINT to +MAXINT shall be values of the integer-type.

(b) Any monadic operation performed on an integer value in this interval shall be correctly performed according to the mathematical rules for integer arithmetic.

(c) Any dyadic integer operation on two integer values in this same interval shall be correctly performed according to the mathematical rules for integer arithmetic, provided that the result is also in this interval.

(d) Any relational operation on two integer values in this same interval shall be correctly performed according to the mathematical rules for integer arithmetic.

The results of the real arithmetic operators and functions shall be approximations to the corresponding mathematical results. The accuracy of this approximation shall be implementation-defined.

It shall be an error if an integer operation or function is not performed according to the mathematical rules for integer arithmetic. [96]

6.7.2.3 *Boolean Operators.* Operands and results for Boolean operations shall be of Boolean-type. Boolean operators *or, and,* and *not* shall denote respectively the logical operations of disjunction, conjunction and negation.

Boolean-expression = expression

A Boolean-expression shall be an expression that denotes a value of Boolean-type.

6.7.2.4 *Set Operators.* The types of operands and results for set operations shall be as shown in Table 4.

TABLE 4
Set Operations

Operator	Operation	Type of Operands	Type of Result
+	set union	(1)	same as the operands
−	set difference	(1)	same as the operands
*	set intersection	(1)	same as the operands

(1) a canonical set-of-T type (see 6.7.1)

6.7.2.5 *Relational-Operators.* The types of operands and results for relational operations shall be as shown in Table 5.

The operands of =, <>, <, >, >=, and <= shall be either of compatible types, the same canonical set-of-T type, [97] or one operand shall be of real-type and the other shall be of integer-type.

The operators =, <>, <, and > shall stand for *equal to, not equal to, less than,* and *greater than* respectively.

Except when applied to sets, the operators <= and >= shall stand for *less than or equal to* and *greater than or equal to* respectively.

96. When any operation leads to a value outside the range −MAXINT to MAXINT, the language makes no guarantee on the arithmetic.

97. Two set operands need only have the same host type.

TABLE 5
Relational Operations

Operator	Type of Operands	Type of Result
= <>	any simple, pointer or string-type or canonical set-of-T type	Boolean-type
< >	any simple or string-type	Boolean-type
<= >=	any simple or string-type or canonical set-of-T type	Boolean-type
in	left operand: any ordinal type T right operand: a canonical set-of-T type	Boolean-type

Where u and v denote operands of a set-type, u <= v shall denote the inclusion of u in v and u >= v shall denote the inclusion of v in u.

NOTE. Since the Boolean-type is an ordinal-type with false less than true, then if p and q are operands of Boolean-type, p = q denotes their equivalence and p <= q means p implies q.

When the relational operators =, <>, <, >, <=, and >= are used to compare operands of compatible [98] string-types (see 6.4.3.2), they denote lexicographic relations defined below. Lexicographic ordering imposes a total ordering on values of a string-type. If s1 and s2 are two values of compatible string-types, and n denotes the number of components of the compatible string-types, then

s1 = s2   iff for all i in [1..n]: s1[i] = s2[i]

s1 < s2   iff there exists a p in [1..n]:
     (for all i in [1..p−1]: s1,[i] = s2(i)) and s1[p] < s2[p]

The operator *in* shall denote the value TRUE if the value of the operand of ordinal-type is a member of the value of the set-type, otherwise it shall yield the value FALSE.

6.7.3 *Function-designators.*
A function-designator shall specify the activation of the block of the function-block associated with the function-identifier of the function-designator, and shall yield the value of the result of the activation upon completion of the algorithm of the activation; it shall be an error if the result is undefined upon completion of the algorithm. If the function has any formal parameters the function-designator shall contain a list of actual-parameters that shall be bound to their corresponding formal parameters defined in the function-declaration. The correspondence shall be established by the positions of the parameters in the lists of actual and formal parameters respectively. The

98. Two string types are compatible if they have the same number of characters. Notice that

'JACK' < 'JOHN'

is true in all implementations, but the truth or falsity of

'Jack' < 'JACK'

or

'R2-D2' < '2R-2D'

will depend on the implementation-defined ordinal values of the character set.

99. This means that the order of any side-effects that can arise in evaluating actual parameters is implementation dependent.

100. Consider

```
{ -- S, a for statement, contains G }
99:  for I := 1 to 10 do begin
        ...
        goto 99;
        ...
     end

{ -- S is in the same sequence as G }
     ...
     goto 99;
     ...
99:  DOSOMETHINGSPECIAL;
     ...
     goto 99;
     ...

{ -- S is an outer block containing G }
   procedure OUTER;
     procedure ESCAPE;
     begin
        ...
        goto 99;
        ...
     end;
   begin
     ...
99:  DOSOMETHINGSPECIAL;
     ...
   end;
```

These are the only kind of goto's allowed.

number of actual-parameters shall be equal to the number of formal parameters. The types of the actual-parameters shall correspond to the types of the formal parameters as specified by 6.6.3. The order of evaluation, accessing and binding of the actual-parameters shall be implementation-dependent. **99**

function-designator	=	function-identifier [actual-parameter-list]
actual-parameter-list	=	(actual-parameter [, actual-parameter]...)
actual-parameter	=	expression
	|	variable-access
	|	procedure-identifier
	|	function-identifier

Examples:
```
SUM(A, 63)
GCD(147, K)
SIN(X + Y)
EOF(F)
ORD(F↑)
```

6.8 STATEMENTS

6.8.1 *General.* Statements shall denote algorithmic actions, and shall be executable.

NOTE. Statements may be prefixed by a label.

A label, if any, of a statement S shall be designated as prefixing S, and shall be allowed to occur in a goto-statement G (see 6.8.2.4) if and only if any of the following three conditions is satisfied. **100**

(a) S contains G.

(b) S is a statement of a statement-sequence containing G.

(c) S is a statement of the statement-sequence of the compound-statement of the statement-part of a block containing G.

statement	=	[label :] simple-statement
	|	[label :] structured-statement

NOTE. A goto-statement within a block may refer to a label in an enclosing block, provided that the label prefixes a simple-statement or structured-statement at the outermost level of nesting of the block.

6.8.2 *Simple Statements*

6.8.2.1 *General.* A simple-statement shall be a statement not containing a statement. An empty-statement shall contain no symbol and shall denote no action.

```
simple-statement    = empty-statement | assignment-statement
                    | procedure-statement | goto-statement
empty-statement101 =
```

6.8.2.2 *Assignment-Statements.* An assignment-statement shall attribute the value of the expression of the assignment-statement either to the variable denoted by the variable-access of the assignment-statement, or to the activation result that is denoted by the function-identifier of the assignment-statement; the value shall be assignment-compatible with the type possessed, respectively, by the variable or by the activation result. The function-block associated (see 6.6.2) with the function-identifier of an assignment-statement shall contain the assignment-statement.

```
assignment-statement = variable-access := expression
                     | function-identifier := expression
```

The decision as to the order of accessing the variable and evaluating the expression shall be implementation-dependent; the access shall establish a reference to the variable during the remaining execution of the assignment-statement.102

The state of a variable or activation result when the variable or activation result does not have attributed to it a value specified by its type shall be designated *undefined*. If a variable possesses a structured-type, the state of the variable when every component of the variable is totally-undefined shall be designated *totally-undefined*. Totally-undefined shall be synonymous with undefined for an activation result or a variable that does not possess a structured-type.

Examples:
```
X := Y + Z
P := (1 <= I) and (I < 100)
I := SQR(K) - (I * J)
HUE1 := [BLUE, SUCC(C)]
P1↑.MOTHER := TRUE
```

6.8.2.3 *Procedure-Statements.* A procedure-statement shall specify the activation of the block of the procedure-block associated with the procedure-identifier of the procedure-statement. If the procedure has any formal parameters the procedure-statement shall contain an actual-

101. One use of the empty statement is to ease the rule for the placement of semicolons. For instance in

```
begin
   X := 1;
   Y := 1;
   Z := 1 { -- a semicolon can go here }
end
```

a semicolon can appear after the last statement. In this instance the statement sequence is assumed to have four (not three) statements, the last of which is an empty statement.

Another use is in case statements like

```
case WEEKDAY of
   MON:   STARTWORK;
   TUE:   CONTINUE;
   WED:   { -- do nothing };
   THURS: CONTINUE;
   FRI:   TIDYUP
end
```

where WED has an empty statement associated with it.

Watch out, even cases like

```
{ -- Two empty statements }
if I < 10
   then
   else;
CONTINUE
```

are allowed.

102. Once the variable is established, side-effects shall not alter its identity. Consider the assignment:

```
A[I] := SOMEFUNCTION( A[I] )
```

where the function alters the value of I. Here the value of I used on the left side of the assignment may or may not be the same as the value used on the right side. This will depend on when the left side is evaluated.

Similarly, the effect of

```
I := I + F(I)
```

where F modifies I, is implementation-defined.

parameter-list, which is the list of actual-parameters that shall be bound to their corresponding formal parameters defined in the procedure-declaration. The correspondence shall be established by the positions of the parameters in the lists of actual and formal parameters respectively. The number of actual-parameters shall be equal to the number of formal parameters. The types of the actual-parameters shall correspond to the types of the formal parameters as specified by 6.6.3. The order of evaluation, accessing and binding of the actual-parameters shall be implementation-dependent.

The procedure-identifier in a procedure-statement containing a read-parameter-list shall denote the required procedure READ; the procedure-identifier in a procedure-statement containing a readln-parameter-list shall denote the required procedure READLN; the procedure-identifier in a procedure-statement containing a write-parameter-list shall denote the required procedure WRITE; the procedure-identifier in a procedure-statement containing a writeln-parameter-list shall denote the required procedure WRITELN. **103**

103. The various kinds of parameter lists need to be individually itemized since READ and WRITE do not behave quite like programmer declared procedures.

```
procedure-statement  =  procedure-identifier
                     |  procedure-identifier ( actual-parameter-list )
                     |  procedure-identifier ( read-parameter-list )
                     |  procedure-identifier ( readln-parameter-list )
                     |  procedure-identifier ( write-parameter-list )
                     |  procedure-identifier ( writeln-parameter-list )
```

Examples:
```
PRINTHEADING
TRANSPOSE(A, N, M)
BISECT(FCT, -1.0, +1.0, X)
```

6.8.2.4 *Goto-Statements.* A goto-statement shall indicate that further processing is to continue at the program-point denoted by the label in the goto-statement and shall cause the termination of all activations except:

(a) the activation containing the program-point; and

(b) any activation containing the activation-point of an activation required by exceptions (a) or (b) not to be terminated.

```
goto-statement  =  goto label
```

6.8.3 *Structured-statements*

6.8.3.1 *General*

```
structured-statement  =  compound-statement  |  conditional-statement
                      |  repetitive-statement  |  with-statement
statement-sequence    =  statement [ ; statement ]...
```

The execution of a statement-sequence shall specify the execution of the statements of the statement-sequence in textual order, except as modified by execution of a goto-statement.

6.8.3.2 *Compound-Statements.* A compound-statement shall specify execution of the statement-sequence of the compound-statement.

```
compound-statement =   begin
                          statement-sequence
                       end
```

Example:
```
begin
  Z := X;
  X := Y;
  Y := Z
end
```

6.8.3.3 *Conditional-Statements*

```
conditional-statement  =  if-statement  |  case-statement
```

6.8.3.4 *If-Statements*

```
if-statement = if Boolean-expression then
                 statement
             [ else-part ]
else-part    = else statement
```

If the Boolean-expression of the if-statement yields the value TRUE, the statement of the if-statement shall be executed. If the Boolean-expression yields the value FALSE, the statement of the if-statement shall not be executed and the statement of the else-part (if any) shall be executed.

An if-statement without an else-part shall not be immediately followed by the token *else*.

NOTE. An else-part is thus paired with the nearest preceding otherwise unpaired then. **104**

Examples:
```
(1)    if X < 1.5 then
            Z := X + Y
       else
            Z := 1.5

(2)    if P1 <> nil then
            P1 := P1↑.FATHER
```

104. The pairing of

```
if A > B then
if C > D then
    DOTHIS
else
    DOTHAT
```

shall be

```
if A > B then begin
    if C > D then
        DOTHIS
    else
        DOTHAT
end
```

not

```
if A > B then
    if C > D then
        DOTHIS
else
    DOTHAT
```

```
(3)     if J = 0 then
            if I = 0 then
                WRITELN ('INDEFINITE')
            else
                WRITELN ('INFINITE')
        else
            WRITELN (I / J)
```

6.8.3.5 *Case-Statements.* The values denoted by the case-constants of the case-constant-lists of the case-list-elements of a case-statement shall be distinct and of the same ordinal-type as the expression of the case-index of the case-statement. On execution of the case-statement the case-index shall be evaluated. That value shall then specify execution of the statement of the case-list-element closest-containing the case-constant denoting that value. One of the case-constants shall be equal to the value of the case-index upon entry to the case-statement, [105] otherwise it shall be an error.

NOTE. Case-constants are not the same as statement labels.

```
case-statement      =   case case-index of
                            case-list-element [ ;
                            case-list-element]... [ ; ]
                        end

case-list-element   =   case-constant-list : statement
case-index          =   expression
```

Example:
```
case OPERATOR of
    PLUS:  X := X + Y;
    MINUS: X := X - Y;
    TIMES: X := X * Y
end
```

6.8.3.6 *Repetitive-Statements.* Repetitive-statements shall specify that certain statements are to be executed repeatedly.

```
repetitive-statement  =  repeat-statement | while-statement | for-statement
```

6.8.3.7 *Repeat-Statements*

```
repeat-statement  =  repeat
                        statement-sequence
                     until Boolean-expression
```

The statement-sequence of the repeat-statement shall be repeatedly executed (except as modified by the execution of a goto-statement) until the Boolean-expression of the repeat-statement yields the value true on completion of the statement-sequence. The statement-sequence shall be

105. The type of the case index can include values that are not accounted for in the case statement. For instance

```
case COLUMN of
    1, 2, 6:  SETFLAG;
    10, 20:   ADDITEM;
    72:       CLOSEOUT
end
```

as long as the "holes" in the case constants never arise, all will be well.

executed at least once, because the Boolean-expression is evaluated after execution of the statement-sequence.

Example:
```
repeat
   K := I mod J;
   I := J;
   J := K
until J = 0
```

6.8.3.8 *While-Statements*

```
while-statement  =  while Boolean-expression do
                         statement
```

The while-statement

```
while b do
   body
```

shall be equivalent to

```
begin
   if b then
      repeat
         body
      until not (b)
end
```

Examples:
```
(1)      while I > 0 do
            begin
               if ODD(I) then
                  Z := Z * X;
               I := I div 2;
               X := SQR(X)
            end

(2)      while not EOF(F) do
            begin
               PROCESS(F↑);
               GET(F)
            end
```

6.8.3.9 *For-Statements.* The for-statement shall specify that the statement of the for-statement is to be repeatedly executed while a progression of values is attributed to a variable that is designated the control-variable of the for-statement.

```
for-statement   =  for control-variable := initial-value to final-value do
                        statement
                |  for control-variable := initial-value downto final-value do
                        statement
```

control-variable = entire-variable
initial-value   = expression
final-value   = expression

The control-variable shall be an entire-variable whose identifier is declared in the variable-declaration-part of the block closest-containing the for-statement. The control-variable shall possess an ordinal-type, and the initial-value and final-value shall be of a type compatible with this type. **106** The initial-value and the final-value shall be assignment-compatible with the type possessed by the control-variable if the statement of the for-statement is executed. After a for-statement is executed (other than being left by a goto-statement leading out of it) the control-variable shall be undefined. Neither a for-statement nor any procedure-and-function-declaration-part of the block that closest-contains a for-statement shall contain a statement threatening the variable denoted by the control-variable of the for-statement.

A statement S shall be designated as *threatening* **107** a variable V if one or more of the following statements is true.

(a) S is an assignment-statement and V is denoted by the variable-access of S.

(b) S contains an actual variable parameter that denotes V.

(c) S is a procedure-statement that specifies the activation of the required procedure READ or the required procedure READLN, and V is denoted by a variable-access of a read-parameter-list or readln-parameter-list of S.

(d) S is a for-statement and the control-variable of S denotes V.

Apart from the restrictions imposed by these requirements, the for-statement

```
for v := e1 to e2 do
   body
```

shall be equivalent to **108**

```
begin
    TEMP1 := e1;
    TEMP2 := e2;
    if TEMP1 <= TEMP2 then
        begin
            v := TEMP1;
            body
            while v <> TEMP2 do
                begin
                    v := SUCC(v);
                    body
                end
        end
end
```

106. Notice that

```
for LETTER := 'A' to 'P' do
   { -- some statement }
```

is allowed, since characters have an ordinal type. Notice also that the control variable LETTER must be declared in the same block as the for statement.

107. Things like

```
for X := 1 to 100 do begin
  ...
  X := X + 1;    { -- (a) }
  ...
  UPDATE(X);     { -- (b) }
  ...
  READ(X);       { -- (c) }
  ...
end
```

are not allowed.

108. The statement

```
for I := MIN to MAX do
  A[I] := B[I] + 1
```

is allowed even if MIN is greater than MAX, in which case the statement is not executed. Watch out, though, even in this case the value of I is undefined after execution of the for statement.

and the for-statement

```
for v := el downto e2 do
    body
```

shall be equivalent to

```
begin
    TEMP1 := el;
    TEMP2 := e2;
    if TEMP1 >= TEMP2 then
        begin
            v := TEMP1;
            body;
            while v <> TEMP2 do
                begin
                    v := PRED(v);
                    body
                end
        end
end
```

where TEMP1 and TEMP2 denote auxiliary variables that the program does not otherwise contain, and that possess the type possessed by the variable v if that type is not a subrange-type; otherwise the host type of the type possessed by the variable v.

Examples:

```
(1)     for I := 2 to 63 do
            if A[I] > MAX then
                MAX := A[I]

(2)     for I := 1 to 10 do
            for J := 1 to 10 do
                begin
                    X := 0;
                    for K := 1 to 10 do
                        X := X + M[I,K] * M2[K,J];
                    M[I,J] := X
                end

(3)     for I := 1 to 10 do
            for J := 1 to I - 1 do
                M[I][J] := 0.0

(4)     for C := BLUE downto RED do
            Q(C)
```

6.8.3.10 *With-Statements*

```
with-statement          =   with record-variable-list do
                                statement
record-variable-list    =   record-variable [ , record-variable ]...
field-designator-identifier  =   identifier
```

109. Consider the variable declarations:

```
var
   YEAR: (GOOD, BAD, INDIFFERENT);
   DATE: record
            YEAR:  0..2000;
            MONTH: 1..12;
            DAY:   1..31
         end;
```

Although the statements

```
YEAR      := GOOD;
DATE.YEAR := 1943;
```

are allowed, the statement

```
with DATE do begin
   YEAR  := GOOD:
   MONTH := MONTH + 1
end
```

is not allowed since

```
YEAR := GOOD
```

is interpreted as

```
DATE.YEAR := GOOD
```

Notice also that

```
with DATE do
   DATE.MONTH := MONTH + 1
```

is allowed and means

```
DATE.MONTH := DATE.MONTH + 1
```

110. Consider the following declaration of a record variable R

```
R: record
     A: record
          X1: INTEGER;
          X2: INTEGER
        end;
     B: record
          Y1: INTEGER;
          Y2: INTEGER
        end
   end
```

As a consequence of the rules, the following statements are not allowed.

A with-statement shall specify the execution of the statement of the with-statement. The occurrence of a record-variable as the only record-variable in the record-variable-list of a with-statement shall constitute a defining-point of each of the field-identifiers associated with components of the record-type possessed by the record-variable as a field-designator-identifier for the region that is the statement of the with-statement; each applied occurrence of a field-designator-identifier shall denote that component of the record-variable that is associated with the field-identifier by the record-type. **109** The record-variable shall be accessed before the statement of the with-statement is executed, and that access shall establish a reference to the variable during the entire execution of the statement of the with-statement.

The statement

```
with v1, v2, ... ,vn do
   s
```

shall be equivalent to **110**

```
with v1 do
   with v2 do
      ...
         with vn do
            s
```

Example:

```
with DATE do
   if MONTH = 12 then
      begin
         MONTH := 1;
         YEAR  := YEAR + 1
      end
   else
      MONTH := MONTH + 1
```

has the same effect on the variable date as

```
if DATE.MONTH = 12 then
   begin
      DATE.MONTH := 1;
      DATE.YEAR  := DATE.YEAR + 1
   end
else
   DATE.MONTH := DATE.MONTH + 1
```

6.9 INPUT AND OUTPUT

6.9.1 *The Procedure READ.* The syntax of the parameter list of READ when applied to a textfile shall be:

read-parameter-list = ([file-variable ,] variable-access
                        [, variable-access]...)

If the file-variable is omitted, the procedure shall be applied to the required textfile INPUT.

The following requirements shall apply for the procedure READ (where f denotes a textfile and v1 ... vn denote variable-accesses possessing the char-type (or a subrange of char-type), the integer-type (or a subrange of integer-type), or the real-type).

(a) READ(f, v1, ... ,vn) shall access the textfile variable and establish a reference to that textfile variable for the remaining execution of the statement. The execution of the statement shall be equivalent to

```
begin
    READ(ff, v1);
    READ(ff, v2, ... ,vn)
end
```

where ff denotes the referenced textfile variable. The READ statement containing v1 shall be executed before accessing the variables v2, ... ,vn.

(b) If v is a variable-access possessing the char-type (or subrange thereof), READ(f, v) shall access the textfile variable and establish a reference to that textfile variable for the remaining execution of the statement. The execution of the statement shall be equivalent to

```
begin
    v := ff↑;
    GET(ff)
end
```

where ff denotes the referenced textfile variable.

NOTE. The variable-access is not a variable parameter. Consequently it may be a component of a packed structure and the value of the buffer-variable need only be assignment-compatible with it.

(c) If v is a variable-access possessing the integer-type (or subrange thereof), READ(f, v) shall access the textfile variable and establish a reference to that textfile variable for the remaining execution of the statement. The remaining execution of the statement shall cause the reading from the referenced textfile variable of a sequence of characters. Preceding spaces and end-of-lines shall be skipped. It shall be an error if the rest of the sequence does not form a signed-integer according to the syntax of 6.1.5. Reading shall cease as soon as the buffer-variable of the referenced textfile does not have attributed to it a character contained by the signed-integer. The value of the signed-integer thus read shall be assignment-compatible with the type possessed by v, and shall be attributed to v.

```
{ -- R.X1 is incorrect }
with R do
    X1 := 1

{ -- wrong order of A and R }
with A, R do
    X1 := 1
```

but

```
{ -- a record variable }
with R.A do
    X1 := 1   { -- means R.A.X1 }

{ -- nested records }
with R, A do
    X1 := 1   { -- means R.A.X1 }

{ -- can also use R, B, A }
with R, A, B do begin
    X1 := 1;   { -- means R.A.X1 }
    Y1 := 1    { -- means R.B.Y1 }
end
```

are allowed. Now suppose that the definition of B were changed to

```
B: record
    X1: INTEGER;
    X2: INTEGER
   end
```

making A and B have the same field identifiers. Then we would have

```
with R, A, B do
    X1 := 1   { -- means R.B.X1 }
```

which is not the same as

```
with R, B, A do
    X1 := 1   { -- means R.A.X1 }
```

(d) If v is a variable-access possessing the real-type, READ(f, v) shall access the textfile variable and establish a reference to that textfile variable for the remaining execution of the statement. The remaining execution of the statement shall cause the reading from the referenced textfile variable of a sequence of characters. Preceding spaces and end-of-lines shall be skipped. It shall be an error if the rest of the sequence does not form a signed-number according to the syntax of 6.1.5. Reading shall cease as soon as the buffer-variable of the referenced textfile does not have attributed to it a character contained by the signed-number. The value denoted by the number thus read shall be attributed to the variable v.

(e) When READ is applied to f, it shall be an error if the buffer-variable f↑ is undefined or the pre-assertions [111] for GET do not hold (see 6.4.3.5).

6.9.2 *The Procedure READLN.* The syntax of the parameter list of READLN shall be:

readln-parameter-list   =   [(file-variable [, variable-access]...)]
                          | [(variable-access [, variable-access]...)]

READLN shall only be applied to textfiles. If the file-variable or the entire readln-parameter-list is omitted, the procedure shall be applied to the required textfile INPUT.

READLN(f, v1, ... ,vn) shall access the textfile variable and establish a reference to that textfile variable for the remaining execution of the statement. The execution of the statement shall be equivalent to

```
begin
   READ(ff, v1, ... ,vn);
   READLN(ff)
end
```

where ff denotes the referenced textfile variable.

READLN(f) shall access the textfile variable and establish a reference to that textfile variable for the remaining execution of the statement. The execution of the statement shall be equivalent to

```
begin
   while not EOLN(ff) do
      GET(ff);
   GET(ff)
end
```

where ff denotes the referenced textfile variable.

111. For example, the file must be in reading (Inspection) mode. Thus a file cannot be used simultaneously for both input and output.

NOTE. The effect of READLN is to place the current file position just past the end of the current line in the textfile. Unless this is the end-of-file position, the current file position is therefore at the start of the next line.

6.9.3 *The Procedure WRITE.* The syntax of the parameter list of WRITE when applied to a textfile shall be:

write-parameter-list = ([file-variable ,] write-parameter
                             [, write-parameter]...)
write-parameter   = expression [: expression [: expression]]

If the file-variable is omitted, the procedure shall be applied to the required textfile OUTPUT. When WRITE is applied to a textfile f, it shall be an error if f is undefined or f.M = Inspection (see 6.4.3.5). An application of WRITE to a textfile f shall cause the buffer-variable f↑ to become undefined.

WRITE(f, p1, ... ,pn) shall access the textfile variable and establish a reference to that textfile variable for the remaining execution of the statement. The execution of the statement shall be equivalent to

```
begin
    WRITE(ff, p1);
    WRITE(ff, p2, ... ,pn)
end
```

where ff denotes the referenced textfile variable. The WRITE statement containing p1 shall be executed before evaluating the write-parameters p2, ... ,pn.

6.9.3.1 *Write-Parameters.* The write-parameters p shall have the following forms:

e : TotalWidth : FracDigits
e : TotalWidth
e

where e is an expression whose value is to be written on the file f and may be of integer-type, real-type, char-type, Boolean-type or a string-type, and where TotalWidth and FracDigits are expressions of integer-type whose values are the field-width parameters. The values of TotalWidth and FracDigits shall be greater than or equal to one; it shall be an error if either value is less than one.[112]

WRITE(f, e) shall be equivalent to the form WRITE(f, e: TotalWidth), using a default value for TotalWidth that depends on the type of e; for integer-type, real-type and Boolean-type the default values shall be implementation-defined.

112. Some examples (the quotes are not printed):

```
{ -- Right justification }
WRITE ('A': 5)          "    A"

{ -- TotalWidth can be exceeded }
WRITE ('$', 3: 2)       "$ 3"
WRITE ('$', 33: 2)      "$33"
WRITE ('$', 333: 2)     "$333"

{ -- A minus sign must be printed }
WRITE (-99: 5)          "  -99"
WRITE (-99: 2)          "-99"

{ -- Assuming an integer has a default width of 10 }
WRITE (99)              "        99"

{ -- Assuming an exponent has 2 digits }
WRITE (12.34: 12)       " 1.23400E+01"
WRITE (-12.34: 12)      "-1.23400E+01"
WRITE (12.34: 2)        " 1.2E+01"

{ -- Zeros are filled to the right }
WRITE (12.34: 8: 3)     "  12.340"
WRITE(-12.34: 8: 3)     " -12.340"

{ -- Fractional digits can be truncated }
WRITE (12.34: 2: 1)     "12.3"
WRITE (12.34: 8: 1)     "    12.3"

{ -- TRUE is treated like a string }
WRITE (TRUE)            "TRUE"
WRITE (TRUE: 6)         "  TRUE"

{ -- Strings can be truncated }
WRITE ('THIS': 2)       "TH"
```

Notice that

```
WRITE (I*25 : 10 : 2)
```

where I is an integer, is not allowed. Such an expression must be of real-type. Changing it to

```
WRITE (I * 25.0 : 10 : 2)
```

is fine.

WRITE(f, e: TotalWidth: FracDigits) shall be applicable only if e is of real-type (see 6.9.3.4.2). **113**

6.9.3.2 *Char-Type.* If e is of char-type, the default value of TotalWidth shall be one. The representation written on the file f shall be:

(TotalWidth − 1) spaces,
the character value of e.

6.9.3.3 *Integer-Type.* If e is of integer-type, the decimal representation of e shall be written on the file f. Assume a function

```
function INTEGERSIZE (X: INTEGER): INTEGER;
   { -- Returns the number of digits, Z, such that
      -- 10 to the power (Z-1) <= ABS(X) < 10 to the power Z }
```

and let INTDIGITS be the positive integer defined by:

```
if e = 0 then
   INTDIGITS := 1
else
   INTDIGITS := INTEGERSIZE(e);
```

then the representation shall consist of:

(a) if TotalWidth >= INTDIGITS + 1;
   (TotalWidth − INTDIGITS − 1) spaces,
   the sign character: − if e < 0, otherwise a space,
   INTDIGITS digit-characters of the decimal representation
   of ABS(e).

(b) If TotalWidth < INTDIGITS + 1:
   if e < 0 the sign character −,
   INTDIGITS digit-characters of the decimal representation
   of ABS(e).

6.9.3.4 *Real-Type.* If e is of real-type, a decimal representation of the number e, rounded to the specified number of significant figures or decimal places, shall be written on the file f.

6.9.3.4.1 *The Floating-Point Representation.* WRITE(f, e: TotalWidth) shall cause a floating-point representation of e to be written. Assume functions

```
function TENPOWER (INT: INTEGER): REAL;
   { -- Returns 10.0 raised to the power INT }
```

```
function REALSIZE (Y: REAL): INTEGER;
   { -- Returns the value, z, such that
     -- TENPOWER(Z - 1) <= ABS(Y) < TENPOWER(Z) }

function TRUNCATE (Y: REAL; DECPLACES: INTEGER): REAL;
   { -- Returns the value of Y after truncation to
     -- DECPLACES decimal places }
```

let EXPDIGITS be an implementation-defined value representing the number of digit-characters written in an exponent:

let ACTWIDTH be the positive integer defined by:

```
if TotalWidth >= EXPDIGITS + 6 then
   ACTWIDTH := TotalWidth
else
   ACTWIDTH := EXPDIGITS + 6;
```

and let the non-negative number EWRITTEN, the positive integer DECPLACES and the integer EXPVALUE be defined by:

```
DECPLACES := ACTWIDTH - EXPDIGITS - 5;
if e = 0.0 then
   begin
      EWRITTEN := 0.0;
      EXPVALUE := 0
   end
else
   begin
      EWRITTEN := ABS(e);
      EXPVALUE := REALSIZE(EWRITTEN) - 1;
      EWRITTEN := EWRITTEN / TENPOWER(EXPVALUE);
      EWRITTEN := EWRITTEN + 0.5 * TENPOWER(-DECPLACES);
      if EWRITTEN <= 10.0 then
         begin
            EWRITTEN := EWRITTEN / 10.0;
            EXPVALUE := EXPVALUE + 1
         end;
      EWRITTEN := TRUNCATE(EWRITTEN, DECPLACES)
   end;
```

then the floating-point representation of the value of e shall consist of: 114

the sign character (- if (e < 0) and (EWRITTEN > 0), otherwise a space),
the leading digit-character of the decimal representation of EWRITTEN,
the character .,
the next DECPLACES digit-characters of the decimal representation of EWRITTEN,
an implementation-defined exponent character (either e or E),
the sign of EXPVALUE (- if EXPVALUE < 0, otherwise +),
the EXPDIGITS digit-characters of the decimal representation of EXPVALUE (with leading zeros if the value requires them).

114. Consider the call

```
WRITE (-123.4 : 11)
```

where numbers are written with two-digit exponents. Here

```
TotalWidth = 11
EXPDIGITS  = 2
ACTWIDTH   = 11
DECPLACES  = 4
```

The algorithm for computing EWRITTEN first takes the absolute value of e (123.4) and sets

```
EXPVALUE = 2
```

Then it successively sets EWRITTEN to 1.234 and 1.23405. After truncation, EWRITTEN becomes 1.2340. The printed value is

```
-1.2340E+02
```

6.9.3.4.2 *The Fixed-Point Representation.* WRITE(f, e: TotalWidth: FracDigits) shall cause a fixed-point representation of e to be written. Assume the functions TENPOWER and TRUNCATE described in 6.9.3.4.1;

let EWRITTEN be the non-negative number defined by:

```
if e = 0.0 then
   EWRITTEN := 0.0
else
   begin
      EWRITTEN := ABS(e);
      EWRITTEN := EWRITTEN + 0.5 * TENPOWER(- FracDigits);
      EWRITTEN := TRUNCATE(EWRITTEN, FracDigits)
   end;
```

let INTDIGITS be the positive integer defined by:

```
if REALSIZE(EWRITTEN) < 1 then
   INTDIGITS := 1
else
   INTDIGITS := REALSIZE(EWRITTEN);
```

and let MINNUMCHARS be the positive integer defined by:

```
MINNUMCHARS := INTDIGITS + FracDigits + 1;
if (e < 0.0) and (EWRITTEN > 0) then
   MINNUMCHARS := MINNUMCHARS + 1;   { - required ]
```

then the fixed-point representation of the value of e shall consist of:

if TotalWidth >= MINNUMCHARS, (TotalWidth – MINNUMCHARS) spaces,
the character – if (e <) and (EWRITTEN > 0),
the first INTDIGITS digit-chaacters of the decimal representation of the value of EWRITTEN,
the character .,
the next FracDigits digit-characters of the decimal representation of the value of EWRITTEN.

NOTE. At least MINNUMCHARS characters are written. If TotalWidth is less than this value, no initial spaces are written.

6.9.3.5 *Boolean-Type.* If e is of Boolean-type, a representation of the word true or the word false (as appropriate to the value of e) shall be written on the file f. This shall be equivalent to writing the appropriate character-strings TRUE or FALSE (see 6.9.3.6), where the case of each letter is implementation-defined, with a field-width parameter of TotalWidth.

6.9.3.6 *String-Types.* If the value of e is a string-type with n components, the default value of TotalWidth shall be n. The representation shall consist of:

if TotalWidth > n

(TotalWidth – n) spaces,

the first through n-th characters of the value of e in that order.

if 1 <= TotalWidth <= n,

the first through TotalWidth-th characters in that order.[115]

115. Unlike other types, character strings that exceed TotalWidth are truncated, for example

```
WRITE ('ABCDEF' : 3)
```

prints

```
ABC
```

6.9.4 *The Procedure WRITELN.* The syntax of the parameter list of WRITELN shall be:

writeln-parameter-list = [(file-variable [, write-parameter]...)]
                         | [(write-parameter [, write-parameter]...)]

WRITELN shall only be applied to textfiles. If the file-variable or the writeln-parameter-list is omitted, the procedure shall be applied to the required textfile OUTPUT.

WRITELN(f, p1, ... ,pn) shall access the textfile variable and establish a reference to that textfile variable for the remaining execution of the statement. The execution of the statement shall be equivalent to

```
begin
    WRITE(ff, p1, ..., pn);
    WRITELN(ff)
end
```

where ff denotes the referenced textfile variable.

WRITELN shall be defined by a pre-assertion and a post-assertion using the notation of 6.6.5.2.

pre-assertion (f0 is not undefined) and (f0.M = Generation) and (f0.R = S()).

post-assertion (f.L = (f0.L $\cdot$ S(e))) and
(f↑ is totally-undefined) and
(f.R = S()) and (f.M = Generation),
where S(e) is the sequence consisting solely of the end-of-line component defined in 6.4.3.5.

NOTE. WRITELN(f) terminates the partial line, if any, which is being generated. By the conventions of 6.6.5.2 it is an error if the pre-assertion is not true prior to WRITELN(f).

6.9.5 *The Procedure PAGE.* It shall be an error if the pre-assertion required for WRITELN(f) (see 6.9.4) does not hold prior to the activation of PAGE(f). If the actual-parameter-list is omitted the procedure shall be applied to the required textfile OUTPUT. PAGE(f) shall cause an implementation-defined effect on the textfile f, such that subsequent text written to f will be on a new page if the textfile is printed on a suitable device, shall perform an implicit WRITELN(f) if f.L is not empty and if f.L.last is not the end-of-line component (see 6.4.3.5), and shall cause the buffer-variable f↑ to become totally-undefined. The effect of inspecting a textfile to which the PAGE procedure was applied during generation shall be implementation-dependent.

6.10 PROGRAMS

program	=	program-heading ; program-block .
program-heading	=	program identifier [(program-parameters)]
program-parameters	=	identifier-list
program-block	=	block

The identifier of the program-heading shall be the program name that shall have no significance within the program.[116] The identifiers contained by the program-parameters shall be distinct and shall be designated program parameters. Each program parameter shall have a defining-point as a variable-identifier for the region that is the program-block. The binding of the variables denoted by the program parameters to entities external to the program shall be implementation-dependent, except if the variable possesses a file-type in which case the binding shall be implementation-defined.

NOTE. The external representation of such external entities is not defined by this standard, nor is any property of a Pascal program dependent on such representation.[117]

The occurrence of the required identifier INPUT or the required identifier OUTPUT as a program parameter shall constitute its defining-point for the region that is the program-block as a variable-identifier of the required type denoted by the required type-identifier TEXT. Such occurrence of the identifier INPUT shall cause the post-assertions of RESET to hold, and of OUTPUT, the post-assertions of REWRITE to hold, prior to the first access to the textfile or its associated buffer-variable. The effect of the application of the required procedure RESET or the required procedure REWRITE to either of these textfiles shall be implementation-defined.[118]

Examples:

(1)
```
program COPY (F, G);
    var
        F, G: file of REAL;
begin
    RESET(F);
    REWRITE(G);
    while not EOF(F) do begin
        G↑ := f↑;
        GET(F);
        PUT(G)
    end
end
```

116. Thus
```
program REUSENAME;
    var
        REUSENAME: INTEGER;
begin
    ...
end
```
is allowed.

117. Usually the program parameters will be files, but this is not required. A heading like
```
program GETMEDIAN (DATAFILE, MEDIAN);
```
where MEDIAN is an integer variable, is allowed.

118. The required files INPUT and OUTPUT are not declared in the declaration part of the program. The file INPUT is assumed to be reset (ready for reading) and the file OUTPUT assumed to be rewritten (ready for writing). The exact effect of RESET and REWRITE is implementation defined. For instance, if the file INPUT is associated with an interactive terminal, an implementation may forbid application of REWRITE. If the file OUTPUT is associated with a printer, an implementation may define RESET as having no effect.

(2)
```
program COPYTEXT (INPUT, OUTPUT);
{ -- This program copies the characters and line structure of the
  -- textfile INPUT to the textfile OUTPUT. }
    var
        CH: CHAR;
begin
    while not EOF do begin
        while not EOLN do begin
            READ(CH);
            WRITE(CH)
        end;
        READLN;
        WRITELN
    end
end
```

(3)
```
program T6P6P3P4 (OUTPUT);
    var
        GLOBALTWO: INTEGER:

    procedure DUMMY;
    begin
        WRITELN('FAIL4')
    end { -- of dummy };

    procedure P (procedure F(procedure FF; procedure GG);  procedure G);
        var
            LOCALTOP: INTEGER;

        procedure R;
        begin
            if GLOBALONE = 1 then
                begin
                    if (GLOBALTWO <> 2) or (LOCALTOP <> 1) then
                        WRITELN('FAIL1')
                end
            else if GLOBALONE = 2 then
                begin
                    if (GLOBALTWO <> 2) or (LOCALTOP <> 2) then
                        WRITELN('FAIL2')
                    else
                        WRITELN('PASS')
                end
            else
                WRITELN('FAIL3');
            GLOBALONE := GLOBALONE + 1
        end { -- of R };
```

119. This is a good example, full of tricks. The key to understanding this program is the activation record associated with an actual parameter that is a procedure. Notice first that procedure P is called recursively. This gives rise to two instantiations of LOCALTOP. Next notice that in the recursive call to P the actual parameter R is associated with the pairing of LOCALTOP equal to 1. When P is entered in its recursive call, it in turn will give rise to the call

F(G, R)

where F is linked with Q and G is linked with R, i.e. we have

Q(R,R)

This is the key call. The left occurrence of R has an activation record where LOCALTOP is 1, the right occurrence has an activation where LOCALTOP is 2. Good luck.

```
              begin { -- of P }
                 GLOBALTWO := GLOBALTWO + 1;
                 LOCALTOP  := GLOBALTWO;
                 if GLOBALTWO = 1 then
                    P(F, R)
                 else
                    F(G, R)
              end { -- of P };

              procedure Q (procedure F;   procedure G);
              begin
                 F;
                 G
              end { -- of Q };

     begin
        GLOBALONE := 1;
        GLOBALTWO := 0;
        P(Q, DUMMY)
     end
```

APPENDICES

APPENDIX A
Collected Syntax

The non-terminal symbols pointer-type, program, signed-number, simple-type, special-symbol and structured-type are only referenced by the semantics and are not used in the right-hand-side of any production. The non-terminal symbol *program* is the start symbol of the grammar.

actual-parameter	=	expression | variable-access
	|	procedure-identifier | function-identifier
actual-parameter-list	=	(actual-parameter [, actual-parameter]...)
adding-operator	=	+ | – | or
apostrophe-image	=	''
array-type	=	array "[" index-type [, index-type]... "]" of component-type
array-variable	=	variable-access
assignment-statement	=	variable-access := expression
	|	function-identifier := expression
base-type	=	ordinal-type
block	=	label-declaration-part
		constant-definition-part
		type-definition-part
		variable-declaration-part
		procedure-and-function-declaration-part
		statement-part
Boolean-expression	=	expression
buffer-variable	=	file-variable ↑
case-constant	=	constant
case-constant-list	=	case-constant [, case-constant]...
case-index	=	expression

case-list-element	=	case-constant-list : statement
case-statement	=	case case-index of
		case-list-element [;
		case-list-element]... [;
		end
character-string	=	"'" string-element [string-element]... "'"
component-type	=	type-denoter
component-variable	=	indexed-variable | field-designator
compound-statement	=	begin
		statement-sequence
		end
conditional-statement	=	if-statement | case-statement
constant	=	[sign] unsigned-number
	|	[sign] constant-identifier
	|	character-string
constant-definition	=	identifier = constant
constant-definition- part	=	[const constant-definition ;] [constant-definition ;]...]
constant-identifier	=	identifier
control-variable	=	entire-variable
digit	=	0 | 1 | 2 | 3 | 4 | 5 | 6 | 7 | 8 | 9
digit-sequence	=	digit [digit]...
directive	=	letter [letter | digit]...
domain-type	=	type-identifier
else-part	=	else statement
empty-statement	=	
entire-variable	=	variable-identifier
enumerated-type	=	(identifier-list)
expression	=	simple-expression [relational-operator simple-expression]
factor	=	variable-access | unsigned-constant
	|	function-designator | set-constructor
	|	(expression) | not factor

| field-designator | = | record-variable . field-specifier |
| | | field-designator-identifier |

| field-designator-
identifier | = | identifier |

| field-identifier | = | identifier |

| field-list | = | [fixed-part [; variant-part] [;]] |
| | | [variant-part [;]] |

| field-specifier | = | field-identifier |

| file-type | = | file of component-type |

| file-variable | = | variable-access |

| final-value | = | expression |

| fixed-part | = | record-section [; record-section]... |

| for-statement | = | for control-variable := initial-value to final-value do statement |
| | | for control-variable := initial-value downto final-value do statement |

| formal-parameter-list | = | (formal-parameter-section [; formal-parameter-section]...) |

formal-parameter- section	=	value-parameter-specification
		variable-parameter-specification
		procedural-parameter-specification
		functional-parameter-specification

| fractional-part | = | digit-sequence |

| function-block | = | block |

function-declaration	=	function-heading ; directive
		function-identification ; function-block
		function-heading ; function-block

| function-designator | = | function-identifier [actual-parameter-list] |

| function-heading | = | function identifier [formal-parameter-list] : result-type |

| function-identification | = | function function-identifier |

| function-identifier | = | identifier |

| functional-parameter-
specification | = | function-heading |

| goto-statement | = | goto label |

identified-variable	=	pointer-variable ↑
identifier	=	letter [letter | digit]...
identifier-list	=	identifier [, identifier]...
if-statement	=	if Boolean-expression then statement [else-part]
index-expression	=	expression
index-type	=	ordinal-type
indexed-variable	=	array-variable "[" index-expression [, index-expression]... "]"
initial-value	=	expression
label	=	digit-sequence
label-declaration-part	=	[label label [, label]... ;]
letter	=	A | B | C | D | E | F | G | H | I | J | K | L | M | N | O | P | Q | R | S | T | U | V | W | X | Y | Z
member-designator	=	expression [.. expression]
multiplying-operator	=	* | / | div | mod | and
new-ordinal-type	=	enumerated-type | subrange-type
new-pointer-type	=	↑ domain-type
new-structured-type	=	[packed] unpacked-structured-type
new-type	=	new-ordinal-type | new-structured-type | new-pointer-type
ordinal-type	=	new-ordinal-type | ordinal-type-identifier
ordinal-type-identifier	=	type-identifier
pointer-type	=	new-pointer-type | pointer-type-identifier
pointer-type-identifier	=	type-identifier
pointer-variable	=	variable-access
procedural-parameter-specification	=	procedure-heading
procedure-and-function-declaration-part	=	[procedure-or-function-declaration]...

procedure-block	=	block
procedure-declaration	=	procedure-heading ; directive
	|	procedure-identification ; procedure-block
	|	procedure-heading ; procedure-block
procedure-or-function- declaration	=	procedure-declaration | function-declaration
procedure-heading	=	procedure identifier [formal-parameter-list]
procedure- identification	=	procedure procedure-identifier
procedure-identifier	=	identifier
procedure-statement	=	procedure-identifier
	|	procedure-identifier (actual-parameter-list)
	|	procedure-identifier (read-parameter-list)
	|	procedure-identifier (readln-parameter-list)
	|	procedure-identifier (write-parameter-list)
	|	procedure-identifier (writeln-parameter-list)
program	=	program-heading ; program-block
program-block	=	block
program-heading	=	program identifier [(program-parameters)]
program-parameters	=	identifier-list
read-parameter-list	=	([file-variable,] variable-access [, variable-access]...)
readln-parameter-list	=	[(file-variable [, variable-access]...)]
	|	[(variable-access [, variable-access]...)]
real-type-identifier	=	type-identifier
record-section	=	identifier-list : type-denoter
record-type	=	record
		field-list
		end
record-variable	=	variable-access
record-variable-list	=	record-variable [, record-variable]...
relational-operator	=	= | <> | < | > | <= | >= | in
repeat-statement	=	repeat
		statement-sequence
		until Boolean-expression

repetitive-statement	=	repeat-statement | while-statement | for-statement
result-type	=	simple-type-identifier | pointer-type-identifier
scale-factor	=	signed-integer
set-constructor	=	"[" [member-designator [, member-designator]...] "]"
set-type	=	set of base-type
sign	=	+ | –
signed-integer	=	[sign] unsigned-integer
signed-number	=	signed-integer | signed-real
signed-real	=	[sign] unsigned-real
simple-expression	=	[sign] term [adding-operator term]...
simple-statement	=	empty-statement | assignment-statement | procedure-statement | goto-statement
simple-type	=	ordinal-type | real-type-identifier
simple-type-identifier	=	type-identifier
special-symbol	=	+ | – | * | / | = | < | > | [|] | . | , : | ; | ↑ | (|) | <> | <= | >= | := | .. | word-symbol
statement	=	[label :] simple-statement | [label :] structured-statement
statement-part	=	compound-statement
statement-sequence	=	statement [; statement]...
string-character	=	one-of-a-set-of-implementation-defined-characters
string-element	=	apostrophe-image | string-character
structured-statement	=	compound-statement | conditional-statement | repetitive-statement | with-statement
structured-type	=	new-structured-type | structured-type-identifier
structured-type-identifier	=	type-identifier
subrange-type	=	constant .. constant
tag-field	=	identifier
tag-type	=	ordinal-type-identifier

term	=	factor [multiplying-operator factor]...
type-definition	=	identifier = type-denoter
type-definition-part	=	[type type-definition ; [type-definition ;]...]
type-denoter	=	type-identifier | new-type
type-identifier	=	identifier
unpacked-structured- type	=	array-type | record-type | set-type | file-type
unsigned-constant	=	unsigned-number | character-string | constant-identifier | nil
unsigned-integer	=	digit-sequence
unsigned-number	=	unsigned-integer | unsigned-real
unsigned-real	=	unsigned-integer . fractional-part [E scale-factor] | unsigned-integer E scale-factor
value-parameter- specification	=	identifier-list : type-identifier
variable-access	=	entire-variable | component-variable | identifier-variable | buffer-variable
variable-declaration	=	identifier-list : type-denoter
variable-declaration- part	=	[var variable-declaration ; [variable-declaration ;]...]
variable-identifier	=	identifier
variable-parameter- specification	=	var identifier-list : type-identifier
variant	=	case-constant-list : (field-list)
variant-part	=	case variant-selector of variant [; variant]
variant-selector	=	[tag-field :] tag-type
while-statement	=	while Boolean-expression do statement
with-statement	=	with record-variable-list do statement
word-symbol	=	and | array | begin | case | const | div | do | downto | else | end | file | for | function | goto | if | in | label | mod | nil | not | of | or | packed | procedure | program | record | repeat | set | then | to | type | until | var | while | with

write-parameter   =   expression [: expression [: expression]]

write-parameter-list   =   ([file-variable ,] write-parameter [, variable-access]...)

writeln-parameter-list   =   [(file-variable [, write-parameter]...)]
                             [(write-parameter [, write-parameter]...)])

ABS	6.6.6.2
ARCTAN	6.6.6.2
BOOLEAN	6.4.2.2
CHAR	6.4.2.2
CHR	6.6.6.4
COS	6.6.6.2
DISPOSE	6.6.5.3
EOF	6.6.6.5
EOLN	6.6.6.5
EXP	6.6.6.2
FALSE	6.4.2.2
GET	6.6.5.2
INPUT	6.10
INTEGER	6.4.2.2
LEN	6.6.6.2
MAXINT	6.7.2.2
NEW	6.6.5.3
ODD	6.6.6.5
ORD	6.6.6.4
OUTPUT	6.10
PACK	6.6.5.4
PAGE	6.9.5
PRED	6.6.6.4
PUT	6.6.5.2
READ	6.6.5.2, 6.9.1
READLN	6.9.2
REAL	6.4.2.2
RESET	6.6.5.2
REWRITE	6.6.5.2
ROUND	6.6.6.3
SIN	6.6.6.2
SQR	6.6.6.2
SQRT	6.6.6.2
SUCC	6.6.6.4
TEXT	6.4.3.5
TRUE	6.4.2.2
TRUNC	6.6.6.3
UNPACK	6.6.5.4
WRITE	6.6.5.2, 6.9.3
WRITELN	6.9.4

APPENDIX C
Errors

A complying processor is required to provide documentation concerning its treatment of errors. To facilitate the production of such documentation, all the errors specified in Section 6 are described again in this appendix.

1. For an indexed-variable closest-containing a single-index-expression, the value of the index-expression is assignment-compatible with the index-type of the array-type.

2. It is an error unless a variant is active for the entirety of each reference and access to each component of the variant.

3. It is an error if the pointer-variable of an identified-variable denotes a nil-value.

4. It is an error if the pointer-variable of an identified-variable is undefined.

5. It is an error to remove from its pointer-type the identifying-value of an identified variable when a reference to the identified variable exists.

6. It is an error to alter the value of a file-variable f when a reference to the buffer-variable f↑ exists.

7. For a value parameter, the actual-parameter is an expression of an ordinal-type whose value is assignment-compatible with the type possessed by the formal parameter.

8. For a value parameter, the actual-parameter is an expression of a set-type whose value is assignment-compatible with the type possessed by the formal parameter.

9. It is an error if the file mode is not Generation immediately prior to any use of PUT, WRITE, WRITELN or PAGE.

10. It is an error if the file is undefined immediately prior to any use of PUT, WRITE, WRITELN or PAGE.

11. It is an error if end of file is not true immediately prior to any use of PUT, WRITE (or WRITELN or PAGE).

12. It is an error if the buffer-variable is undefined immediately prior to any use of PUT.

13. It is an error if the file is undefined immediately prior to any use of RESET.

14. It is an error if the file mode is not Inspection immediately prior to any use of GET or READ.

15. It is an error if the file is undefined immediately prior to any use of GET or READ.

16. It is an error if end of file is true immediately prior to any use of GET or READ.

17. For READ, the value possessed by the buffer-variable is assignment-compatible with the variable-access.

18. For WRITE, the value possessed by the expression is assignment-compatible with the buffer-variable.

19. For NEW(p,c1, ... ,cn), it is an error if a variant of a variant-part within the new variable becomes active and a different variant of the variant-part is one of the specified variants.

20. For DISPOSE(p), it is an error if the identifying-value had been created using the form NEW(p,c1, ... ,cn).

21. For DISPOSE(p, k1, ... ,km), it is an error if the variable had been created using the form NEW(p,c1, ... ,cn) and m is not equal to n.

22. For DISPOSE(p,k1, ... ,km), it is an error if the variants in the variable identified by the pointer value of p are different from those specified by the case-constants k1, ... ,km.

23. For DISPOSE, it is an error if the parameter of a pointer-type has a nil-value.

24. For DISPOSE, it is an error if the parameter of a pointer-type is undefined.

25. It is an error if a variable created using the second form of NEW is accessed by the identified-variable of the variable-access of a factor, of an assignment-statement, or of an actual-parameter.

26. For PACK, the parameter of ordinal-type is assignment-compatible with the index-type of the unpacked array parameter.

27. For PACK, it is an error if any of the components of the unpacked array are both undefined and accessed.

28. For PACK, it is an error if the index-type of the unpacked array is exceeded.

29. For UNPACK, the parameter of ordinal-type is assignment-compatible with the index-type of the unpacked array parameter.

30. For UNPACK, it is an error if any of the components of the packed array are undefined.

31. For UNPACK, it is an error if the index-type of the unpacked array is exceeded.

32. SQR(x) computes the square of x. It is an error if such a value does not exist.

33. For LN(x), it is an error if x is not greater than zero.

34. For SQRT(x), it is an error if x is negative.

35. For TRUNC(x), the value of TRUNC(x) is such that if x is positive or zero then $0 <= x-\text{TRUNC}(x) < 1$; otherwise $-1 < x-\text{TRUNC}(x) <= 0$. It is an error if such a value does not exist.

36. For ROUND(x), if x is positive or zero then ROUND(x) is equivalent to TRUNC(x+0.5), otherwise ROUND(x) is equivalent to TRUNC(x–0.5). It is an error if such a value does not exist.

37. For CHR(x), the function returns a result of char-type which is the value whose ordinal number is equal to the value of the expression x if such a character value exists. It is an error if such a character value does not exist.

38. For SUCC(x), the function yields a value whose ordinal number is one greater than that of x, if such a value exists. It is an error if such a value does not exist.

39. For PRED(x), the function yields a value whose ordinal number is one less than that of x, if such a value exists. It is an error if such a value does not exist.

40. When EOF(f) is activated, it is an error if f is undefined.

41. When EOLN(f) is activated, it is an error if f is undefined.

42. When EOLN(f) is activated, it is an error if EOF(f) is true.

43. An expression denotes a value unless a variable denoted by a variable-access contained by the expression is undefined at the time of its use, in which case that use is an error.

44. A term of the form x/y is an error if y is zero.

45. A term of the form i div j is an error if j is zero.

46. A term of the form i mod j is an error if j is zero or negative.

47. It is an error if an integer operation or function is not performed according to the mathematical rules for integer arithmetic.

48. It is an error if the result of an activation of a function is undefined upon completion of the algorithm of the activation.

49. For an assignment-statement, the expression is of an ordinal-type whose value is assignment-compatible with the type possessed by the variable or function-identifier.

50. For an assignment-statement, the expression is of a set-type whose value is assignment-compatible with the type possessed by the variable.

51. For a case-statement, it is an error if none of the case-constants is equal to the value of the case-index upon entry to the case-statement.

52. For a for-statement, the value of the initial-value is assignment-compatible with the type possessed by the control-variable if the statement of the for-statement is executed.

53. For a for-statement, the value of the final-value is assignment-compatible with the type possessed by the control-variable if the statement of the for-statement is executed.

54. On reading an integer from a textfile, after skipping preceding spaces and end-of-lines, it is an error if the rest of the sequence does not form a signed-integer.

55. On reading an integer from a textfile, the value of the signed-integer read is assignment-compatible with the type possessed by variable-access.

56. On reading a number from a textfile, after skipping preceding spaces and end-of-lines, it is an error if the rest of the sequence does not form a signed-number.

57. It is an error if the buffer-variable is undefined immediately prior to any use of READ.

58. On writing to a textfile, the values of TotalWidth and FracDigits are greater than or equal to one; it is an error if either value is less than one.

INDEX

A

Access
6.5.1, 6.5.3.1, 6.5.3.3, 6.5.5, 6.6.3.3, 6.6.5.2, 6.8.2.2, 6.8.3.10, 6.10

Actual
6.6.3.3, 6.6.3.4, 6.6.3.5, 6.7.3, 6.8.2.3, 6.8.3.9

Actual-parameter
6.6.3.2, 6.6.3.3, 6.6.3.4, 6.6.3.5, 6.6.5.3, 6.7.3

Actual-parameter-list
6.6.6.5, 6.7.3, 6.8.2.3, 6.9.5

Array-type
6.4.3.1, 6.4.3.2, 6.5.3.2

Assignment-compatible
6.4.6, 6.5.3.2, 6.6.3.2, 6.6.5.2, 6.6.5.4, 6.8.2.2, 6.8.3.9, 6.9.1

Assignment-statement
6.2.3.3, 6.6.2, 6.6.5.3, 6.8.2.1, 6.8.2.2, 6.8.3.9

B

Base-type
6.4.3.4, 6.4.5, 6.4.6, 6.7.1

Block
6.2.1, 6.2.3.1, 6,2.3.2, 6.2.3.3, 6.2.3.4, 6.3, 6.4.1, 6.4.2.3, 6.5.1, 6.6.1, 6.6.2, 6.6.3.1, 6.6.3.2, 6.6.3.3, 6.6.3.4, 6.6.3.5, 6.7.3, 6.8.1, 6.8.2.3, 6.8.3.9, 6.10

Body
6.6.1, 6.8.3.8, 6.8.3.9

Boolean-expression
6.7.2.3, 6.8.3.4, 6.8.3.7, 6.8.3.8

Boolean-type
6.4.2.2, 6.7.2.3, 6.7.2.5, 6.9.3.1, 6.9.3.5

Buffer-variable
6.5.1, 6.5.5, 6.6.5.2, 6.9.1, 6.9.3, 6.9.5, 6.10

C

Case-constants
6.4.3.3, 6.6.5.3, 6.8.3.5

Character
6.1.7, 6.1.9, 6.4.2.2, 6.6.6.4, 6.9.1, 6.9.3.2, 6.9.3.3, 6.9.3.4.1, 6.9.3.4.2

Character-string
6.1.1, 6.1.7, 6.1.8, 6.3, 6.4.3.2, 6.7.1

Char-type
6.1.7, 6.4.2.2, 6.4.3.2, 6.4.3.5, 6.5.5, 6.6.6.4, 6.9.1, 6.9.3.1, 6.9.3.2

Closed
6.1.5, 6.1.6, 6.4.6, 6.7.1, 6.7.2.2

Compatible
6.4.3.3, 6.4.5, 6.4.6, 6.4.7, 6.7.2.5, 6.8.3.9

Component
6.4.3.1, 6.4.3.2, 6.4.3.3, 6.4.3.5, 6.5.1, 6.5.3.1, 6.5.3.2, 6.5.3.3, 6.6.2, 6.6.3.3, 6.6.5.2, 6.6.6.5, 6.8.2.2, 6.8.3.10, 6.9.1, 6.9.4, 6.9.5

Components
6.1.7, 6.4.3.1, 6.4.3.2, 6.4.3.3, 6.4.3.5, 6.4.5, 6.5.3.3, 6.6.5.2, 6.8.3.10, 6.9.3.6

Component-type
6.4.3.2, 6.4.3.5, 6.4.6, 6.5.5, 6.6.3.2